MW01169944

Dream-Chasing
From The Margins.

Dream-Chasing

From the Margins

A Memoir in Essays

Mia H. Archer

Warria Publishing Company

ISBN (ebook)   978-1-7360648-0-1

ISBN (print)   978-1-7360648-1-8

Library of Congress Cataloging-in-Publication Data
Name: Mia H. Archer
Title: Dream-Chasing From The Margins

DEDICATION

For my daughters,

Tristen and Nadhirah,

the first non-celebrity Black women

I ever truly admired;

~

For my husband, Howard,

you never blinked, not even once;

~

and for Black women everywhere,

we are the love and guiding light for one another.

TABLE OF CONTENTS

INTRODUCTION

1. I Am A Love-Her
2. The Tradition of Secret-Keeping
3. My Alcohol Addiction Story
4. Turning My Blog Into A Book: Fail
5. We Are Angels, Walking On Earth
6. Getting Over Apologetic Behavior
7. Dream-Chasing Can Crush You Underfoot
8. Courage Not Guaranteed
9. Writing During a National Quarantine
10. Fear As My Ride-or-Die Chick
11. I Leapt—I'm Already Gone
12. Let's Talk About Love!
13. What Kind of Sexy Am I?
14. My Sexual Healing
15. From Zero to Hero With Confidence
16. Renaming Myself Mia
17. Friends Who Happen to Be White
18. The *Black Is King* Film – Am I A Cultural Critic?

19. Happily Married and The Messes In Between

20. Connecting the Dots

Acknowledgements

Appendix

About the Author

You can't connect the dots looking forward; you can only connect them looking backwards. So you have to trust that the dots will somehow connect in your future. You have to trust in something—your gut, destiny, life, karma, whatever. This approach has never let me down, and it has made all the difference in my life.

—Steve Jobs, CEO of Apple, Inc.

INTRODUCTION

I wrote this book for myself because I'd searched and couldn't find a book like this anywhere. I wanted the harder truths about the creative journey: a behind the scenes look, revealing the specifics on struggles common to so many of us. I wanted to understand how I'd gotten so completely lost in the unfolding seasons of my own life story, especially as a Black woman. I wrote my way into understanding.

This book has become the forerunner to another book I'm working on, a book about Black women's friendships. Writing solely about Black women wasn't about exclusion. All women are worthy of their stories, no matter what their complexion or ethnicity. However, I am a Black woman who needed to write her own version of the larger story about the dynamics between us as sisters in skin.

Black women in America are the least prioritized and least protected group in this white male-centric society, otherwise known as the patriarchy. We need as much prioritizing as we can give ourselves. In a world that doesn't always show us love, I think it's essential for us to show ourselves love in as many ways as possible. My way is through writing.

As I investigated the topic of Black women's friendships—approaching women on city streets, in stores, in libraries, in mall parking lots, and other places—I was met with mixed reactions. Quite often, the reactions were emotional. Many of them were positive and pleasant, but also, some were negative and distressing.

Although I was wholly captivated and encouraged by the widespread positive responses, I was also intrigued by the distressing ones. A number of the women surveyed were immediately transparent, providing vulnerable commentary on the topic of friendships. They didn't seem to mind sharing tender recollections of heartbreak from their private chest of memories relating to Black women who'd impacted their lives. Interviews with willing participants—Black women, generous with their time and insight—provided even more evidence of friendships' complexities.

Not only was I unprepared for the emotional responses, but I was also unprepared for the way they would trigger my own emotions and how the triggering would begin to impede my writing progress. I was shaken and I was scared.

When the idea of a book about Black women's friendships found me, I grabbed it because I thought it would be fun. Ha! Sure, we can be fun as individuals in our separate social circles which feel familiar and safe. However, as women who've experienced more than our share of negative drama in society, we can also be extremely hesitant in unfamiliar territories.

Women, in general, are already spectacular and intriguing by virtue of their potential as givers and bringers of human life. But Black women possess something which runs deeper. Like diamonds formed under pressure, in the face of suffering, we continue to not only overcome painful circumstances, many of us thrive. Black women are phenomenal.

And yet, with all our amazing qualities, we are still emotional humans. We hurt.

I knew the friendship topic would bring up memories from my own retired friendships, but I honestly thought the memories would be nostalgic and harmless. I also (naively) thought conversations about friendships would provide opportunities to elevate the more carefree and happier moments shared between Black women. While the friendship stories filled with laughter, joy, and support among the women were plentiful, those kinds of stories tended to be overshadowed by the sadder and more disappointing memories of friendship.

I'd been given all these beautiful friendship stories, and I wasn't sure how to handle them. Of course, the identifying elements of the stories would be changed, and sources would remain anonymous, but it still felt like a challenge.

In addition, I now had to navigate the writing while trying to keep my own emotions in check. I couldn't do it yet. Not back when I first began.

After hitting walls repeatedly during the year and a half I spent working on the manuscript about friendships, I conceded that I had to stop writing and put it aside. The friendship experience among women is just as intimate and tender as a relationship with any love interest, be it partner or spouse. Writing a book about such delicate relationships would take more time. I needed to write a different kind of book first. This book.

As I probed the topic of friendships among us as women, I'd unintentionally touched on sensitive nerves which sparked reminders of buried pain, pain held individually and collectively among us as Black people. In varying degrees, the experience of Blackness in America remains tied to tenuous conditions despite our progress in the face of racism. It seems no matter how far we've gone as a Black race—despite wealth gain and other advancements—none of us are ever completely safe from the insidious undermining pall of racism.

I am a proud novice, writing from the trenches of ordinary people. I don't profess to speak for *all* Black people. I'm telling my own story first because the research into the dynamics among Black women revealed the fact that not only are our friendships fraught, how we behave in the friendship is based on how we view ourselves. These self-perceptions, more often than not, tend to be grounded in faulty belief systems.

But since we never got that far in our discussions—exploring the possibility of faulty roots—I didn't feel comfortable writing about that in the friendship book. However, to omit our belief system's roots—much of our ideas, whether social, religious, or political, has been informed by the overly biased system of patriarchy—was to tell a partial story. Telling a partial story about a component of the Black experience would have been the same to me as lying. And while I don't mind admitting I'm no stranger to telling the occasional lie in my own private life, I didn't want to be culpable as someone memorializing lies in a non-fiction book.

Don't get it twisted, it wasn't as straightforward as I'm explaining it to you now. I did *not* want to write this kind of book at first. A memoir? Hell no! Okay sure, I was a blogger. I already knew what it felt like to share written opinions in a public forum. But this was different. A book like this would need to go deeper with vulnerability. I would have to be more truthful and more transparent than I'd ever been with my writing.

This wasn't what I had in mind when I quit the day job. Not even close. But the idea for this book just would *not* go away. Talk about being even more terrified—*fuck me!* Like it or not, my instincts kept pushing me towards these pages.

I wrote this book despite my reluctance.

In the pages ahead, I unpacked some of my baggage by documenting the writing journey I found myself on. Documenting my experiences was a way of preparing, a way of clearing the mind, and writing my way through the unexpected difficulties met in reflecting on my own Black womanhood. Even though I talk about Blackness, this is not what the book is about. This not a book about Black history or a book about racism. This is a book about one woman's personal journey. As it happens, I'm Black. But my skin color is not all there is to who I am as a person.

This book isn't just a memoir, it's a manifesto and a call to action. I'm standing up to share my version of the Human Story because I finally realize that none of us is less worthy or less important than the next person. As human beings, we're all wired for connection and storytelling is the enjoyable tradition which keeps us connecting.

I got lost along life's way. Writing these pages helped me to find my way back to discovering the woman I truly am. Finding my way back began with the research into Black women friendships.

1

I AM A LOVE-HER

I am a girl who became a woman in a country that hated her.

I saw hate before I fully understood what it was or why I was the recipient of its sizzle.

I was molested and raped by my father. I was (more often than not) hated by my mother for my father's unhealthy obsession with me. By the time I was a teenager, almost a woman, I had realized no one was coming to save me, and I would have to save myself. So I called the police and had my father arrested. For this treacherous act of family betrayal, because I dared to save myself, my entire family—mother, father, brother and, sister— hated me (for a while. I'd felt their wrath: sneers, insults, offensive actions disguised as "mistakes.") because I disrupted everyone's life, even while I saved them from the tyranny of the one man who terrorized us all in a bygone period, during the formative youthful season of our lives. They were confused, I was confused, our world was upside down. There was no manual on how to go forward, having lived this kind of family life. All we knew was our fear and our hate. We had to put it somewhere, so we gathered it up, and we put it first on ourselves, tearing angrily into our own minds and our own hearts, desiring to self-destruct. And then, we put it on each other because it was convenient. We were within striking distance, reflecting our hated selves to one another.

And then, I went out into the world, thinking I might eventually find a safe place, someplace where I could rest and let my guards down. But I was stupefied to discover, the world hated me too. Apparently, while I was busy trying to survive my childhood, racism was alive and well, morphing itself in creative ways beyond its old institutionalized skin.

Who was I? I was broken. I was wounded. I was damaged goods. I had to save myself. But first, I would do everything I could to self-destruct, to implode, to wipe out, and go home because that place they call heaven had to be better than this shithole called life. I wasn't brave enough—or hopeless enough—to do the suicide dance, even though I'd thought about it often. I crawled into a bottle instead. I crawled until addiction wrapped its tentacles around my throat and began a squeeze so subtle, so intoxicating, and so alluring, I said yes, more of this please.

Who am I? I'm a survivor. I'm an overcomer. I am still here. I am a *love-her*, not to be confused with *lover*. Because throughout all of the difficulties I had been facing, throughout all of my life's painful seasons, there was a little girl inside of me who never stopped fighting, never stopped calling out, never stopped begging me to hang on. I learned to *love her*. Loving her, this little girl on the inside, saved my life (repeatedly) and helped me find my way every time I got lost, even if the state of being lost went on for years.

Who am I?

I am a mother who made terrible mistakes during her parenting season, as well as victorious choices on behalf of her children. Being a *love-her* inspired me to love my own two little girls in a nurturing way despite having no examples or precedent for such love in my own life. Being a *love-her* taught me how to place my daughters' needs above my own, watching in awe as my love appeared to help them thrive.

I am a wife to an amazing and beautiful husband after spending years before him choosing all the wrong men, men who regularly broke my heart and amplified my feelings of low self-worth. I am a recovering alcoholic with ten years of sobriety under her bra (I don't wear belts).

I am a writer. Let it be known, although statistically speaking I should have, I did not die. I am still here.

2

THE TRADITION OF SECRET-KEEPING

What's the point of taking our secrets to the grave?

Who does it serve? How has it served any of us so far in life?

I come from a community of secret-keepers. Some of us are especially good at keeping secrets because we were trained to keep secrets from a young age. Now, whenever I think of the girl I was, the one who was prematurely given the burden of secret-keeping by the very adults who should have protected her, it breaks my heart. We can all agree, children are innocents. We hate to see children suffer. And yet, we live in a world whose actions fly in direct conflict with the desire to keep children safe.

My parents wanted me to conceal the fact that they didn't protect us. As a girl, I desperately wanted the approval of these grownups. It didn't matter to me that they hurt me. It only mattered that they approved of me. So when it became clear that our family had secrets they wanted me to protect—even though it felt wrong and filled me with anxiety—I was completely down with protecting the family. I didn't have the forethought to wonder about the endgame. I thought eventually the secret-keeping would make sense. I thought eventually we would all be saved or spared or helped somehow. I figured my parents knew what they were doing.

As I entered young adulthood, I felt the distinctly uncomfortable burden of carrying these secrets. My father was a pedophile/rapist and my mother was his protector. I wasn't supposed to say these things out loud, but I did anyway. I began the telling with a few friends and then with a therapist. But it was still a big secret, and it was poisoning my heart and soul each day I carried it. I didn't know this. I didn't know that the secret I was carrying to protect my family was a seed buried in fertile mind territory which sprouted strong vines of shame, holding me in their clutches.

For a while, I thought it was just us. I thought that my family and I were the only ones struggling with how to move through the world, hiding things we hoped to keep buried. But as I grew older, tuning in more to messages received through community, through entertainment, through media, I realized: oh wait, *everyone* has secrets, and everyone is trying to keep them hidden or buried. This is an actual thing, this taking of secrets to the grave. It wasn't some original master plan that only my parents hatched up.

The World. We were all taking our cues from The World.

I wanted to find a compromise. I wanted to find a compromise because, for a long time, I still believed in the good of The World. I also wanted to find a compromise because these were my parents, my flesh and blood. I still loved them, and in their own way, I believe they had tried to love me too. I wanted to find a way to make our relationship work. But I had to release the secrets: I knew the secret-keeping was killing me slowly.

In my younger days, as I grew into adulthood, I couldn't articulate what was happening. I am writing it all out now, now that time has passed, and I can see things more clearly. The fact is, the secret-keeping was poison to my heart and my mind. The secret-keeping brought shame to live inside and ruin everything I touched. The secret-keeping poisoned every attempt I made at becoming a better person, at trying to live a productive life.

I tried to talk with my parents on several occasions about what had happened in my childhood. They weren't having it. There would be no teary confessions about my parents' own childhood traumas, no concessions about the pain they caused, no amends. The two of them—each time I addressed them, one parent at a time—merely looked at me blankly, as if I were commenting on the rhythm of ocean tides, as if I were talking about something that had absolutely nothing to do with them. And I would let the subject drop. And I would walk away further convinced of my own lunacy.

And so, the compromise became leaving the topic alone. Just forget it. Let's just move on. Have a drink (or dozens of drinks) and move on. I figured, they're old. Who cares? It won't kill me to tuck the whole experience—eleven years of violence and sexual abuse—away into a box of my mind and lock it all up for good. I stopped talking about our shared family secrets.

Besides, now I knew it wasn't just us. Clearly, other families had figured out their own ways to move on. People with secrets go on to live productive lives somehow. Or did they? I honestly didn't know. Who talks about these things? Where is the platform that allows for these kinds of discussions without treating the individuals involved like freaks, without looking at them like aberrations of nature?

This isn't a book about childhood sexual abuse. I didn't want to write that kind of a book. This book is about one writer's journey on her way to pursuing her writing passion full-time. The fact is, books written about uncomfortable subject matters tend to be grouped so they can be deliberately ignored or gawked at by social scientists or peeked into with shame—even while the subjects of said books have nothing they should feel ashamed of—by other former victims like me. So this isn't that kind of a book.

I'm revisiting the choices I made to get to this place, where I've ended up hitting so many unexpected walls on the book writing journey, I had to stop and ask myself just what the hell was going on.

I chose to keep my family's secrets more than I chose to discuss them season after season. Now it was time to face the music with those choices.

What I didn't know when I made that decision is choosing to keep secrets makes you a liar. You become someone who lies by omission, someone who lies by not telling the entire truth about themselves, the entire truth about who they really are. I got that part. I knew that upfront. I was still okay with this because I figured we live in that kind of world anyway, so no biggie. Everybody lies.

But then I went and gave birth on two different occasions to entire human beings who never asked to be born into my web of lies and deceit. And I was like, shit! Now what? I had to decide on which parts of my life were open and which parts would remain closed. It seemed when my children were small that I had plenty of time to figure the secret-keeping/lies/deceit thing out. But time is tricky. One minute time feels like it's dragging, the next minute, it feels like it's speeding by. And it can feel like children go from toddling love-struck groupies who adore you to teenagers giving you the stink-eye stare-down of defiance in nanoseconds when it actually took years. I told my kids *some* things but left other parts out of the telling, and my parenting behavior was oftentimes incongruous with the rules I was laying down for them as offspring.

I take a smidgen of consolation, knowing it wasn't just me and it wasn't just *my* family. It doesn't really help though.

A part of me had died as a result of carrying the family secrets around all these years. Why we continue to live this way in society is a fucking riddle. I don't think I'll ever fully understand it.

I've had to spend all these years feeling deeply ashamed of childhood experiences over which I had absolutely no control. I had no voice and no say. And yet, I was ashamed and embarrassed by this. I got the distinct impression—from my family and social dictates—I was expected to get over my past and move on, I shouldn't look back, and I should definitely keep silent about family secrets. A significant chunk of my life became something to be ashamed of.

When I began my blog (*On Becoming Maria*) in 2017, I did it to give myself courage as a writer. I bared my soul to the readers because I finally understood that there is no shame in having been a victim of sexual abuse. And yet, for those of us—usually women—who experienced sexual assault, shame and guilt tended to be our first response, as if we were co-conspirators in our own debasement. I wrote about my childhood sexual abuse as a way to finally release the shame that had tied up my insides and held me back from dream pursuits for so long.

Yet and still, I was mortified with myself for writing it. While I didn't put specifics about my childhood sexual abuse on the blog, I insisted on writing that this happened. It became a mantra, one I made myself write and speak, as a method of eliminating the physical recoiling, as a way to practice my recall of the helpless feelings without bearing the burden of guilt or shame. Now, when I write the words, *I am a survivor of rape and incest*, it's not much different from writing about reorganizing my closet.

The World has been wrong about its insistence that we take our secrets to the grave. The poison of secret-keeping will (psychically) kill us long before we take our last breath.

Sharing our truths, telling our separate stories is a way of lending courage, calling each other home to our truest and most authentic selves. Telling each other the truth of our experiences is also a way to reveal our shared history of bravery, reminding one another about what's possible if we never give up and what each of us is actually capable of.

3

MY ALCOHOL ADDICTION STORY

I was adrift in the world by age twenty-one.

I didn't feel like I belonged to anyone or any group. I was staring into the abyss of a future of supposedly endless possibilities, and I had no idea what I would do with myself. My parents and I had become like strangers to each other because suddenly we were in new territory; they had no control over me anymore.

I was a college student living on campus two hours away from home.

My joy at being away from home for the first time could not be contained. I was almost manic with good cheer. I quickly found alcohol as the elixir and fuel for good times. It seemed everywhere I looked there was a party. Parties on campus didn't need planning. All it took was a beer run or a liquor store run and an available dorm room. All it took was one student with a willing roommate or one student with an empty dorm room and a few friends. A gathering of two or more bored students with a bottle of wine or tequila between them could suddenly become a party. We didn't even always need music, but music made it more of a party. Someone would eventually press play on a mixtape, word would be passed around in the halls somehow, and other bored students would show up, and the music would get louder.

In those first months of college, it felt like I'd died and gone to heaven. No parents, not even other adults (outside of classes and business hours). Just a bunch of young people, most of us tasting freedom for the first time in our lives, in gleeful and raucous moods, looking to get into lusty trouble or looking to break shit or tear some shit up. Alcohol seemed to be everywhere. Someone always had a red dixie cup with sloshing liquid. And I'd follow the drunkenly raised arm pointing to the room with music or the table with a pitcher or the igloo with melted water and floating beers.

Classes and studying were incidental. I did just enough to pass. I didn't have to show my grades to anyone any longer. I was finally on my own, free to do any foolish thing I chose. I had a wide-open field to blow life up on my own terms this time.

Apparently, while I was partying with my drinking buddies, in a parallel universe, an entire other world of student life, there also existed responsible students who were routinely meeting in the library and holding study groups. Those students weren't drinking and were rarely in attendance at all the parties I'd been busy bouncing around in. On mornings when I was hungover and had dragged myself to a lecture hall thirty minutes late, I would find those same students in their seats looking clear-eyed and keenly alert. This parallel universe became like background noise to me, like dust bunnies in the rooms of partying life. They became afterthoughts, their faces floating before me only after I gawked at my low transcript grades. I knew I needed to get my act together.

Life became surreal during breaks from college life. I experienced conflicting feelings about going home for visits during Christmas and Summer. On one hand, I missed the familiar. I didn't know if my feelings of nostalgia were because friends around me talked about their own home lives, how much they missed a mother or a father, how much they missed a grandmother or a sister, how much they missed a boyfriend or a brother, or an uncle and aunt. Friends around me would pine about favorite foods their mother or grandmother used to cook.

The Normals were suddenly in my life, and I needed to act accordingly. Was I acting? I was torn. I did feel as if I was missing something, something more familiar from my old life than the new life I was living in the moment. There were times when I'd be filled with inexplicable melancholy, even if I didn't know what it was that was making me sad or making me feel like I was missing home. Like my friends, as the time neared for us all to leave for break, I was reminded that this wasn't real life, that this was temporary. Whatever it was that made me feel as if I belonged would vanish when it was time for me to leave this place, and I had no choice but to return to the reality of my true existence.

Back home, my parents and I regarded each other carefully. Putting on our best faces and tentative smiles, we would actually embrace, which gave me the feeling of warm relief and invaded territory all at once. It all felt weird. No one talks about these things enough for me. I had no understanding of how I was supposed to conduct myself. Experiencing the college environment had been a sort of mania like rollercoaster ride meets rollicking concert. And now, I was home. But what was home? It was the place of nightmares unfolding in real life during daylight hours. There were my parents, and even though they'd been monsters who governed my nightmares, I still loved them, and I'd really missed them. How was this possible? How was I supposed to make sense of this and make it fit into my mind to know how to behave? Alcohol was calling, promising an answer.

I did with my parents what I'd learned to do with The Normals in the outside world while pretending to be one of them. I acted *as if* I missed them terribly, and I was delighted to be back home. I acted *as if* being back in our house, seeing our kitchen and the living room, seeing my bedroom again, filled me with utter and relieved happiness. This made my parents smile in relief. They exchanged looks, of course, seeming to arrive at some tacit agreement. It was like they decided I was harmless after all, as if they agreed that I was not only dimwitted but also a little demented. Years later, this would be confirmed for me by my sister and a cousin.

Apparently, the consensus among most of the family was, I was a little off mentally. I wasn't quite balanced or in my right mind. Well, no shit! I was in a lose-lose situation. No one wanted to face the truth of our shared trauma, the fact that we were all violated by our own patriarch, that we were all full of rage we didn't know what to do with. When I had tried to talk about it—being the only one who dared—I was met with immediate backlash, so I zipped my lips evermore.

Well, I guess secret-keepers aren't supposed to smile or act giddy. I guess I went overboard with wanting to give a look of contented acceptance to the family. I should have been pugnacious, I should have looked more like some kind of threat, someone who lived on the side of her foul moods. Perpetual anger is exhausting. I couldn't do it. So the family thought I was soft. But I take consolation in the fact that they also thought I was crazy.

I chose the road of least resistance: I gave them all the silence on the matter of our shared past that they all seemed to want back then. Those years when I'd returned home from college were the years where I would double down on pretense and facades. This was the beginning of my understanding that it was futile to have expectations of my parents that they simply couldn't fulfill. I didn't wrap my head around it immediately, but over time—a few decades—I would come to accept that my parents couldn't give me what they didn't have inside to give. They couldn't love me in the way I needed to be loved. They didn't love themselves. And if they didn't love themselves, there was no way they could possibly love me.

I thought I could accept this about my parents. I thought I could live with their inability—their refusal to figure out how to do their jobs as parents—to show me love. But I couldn't. It broke something at my core, broke it so severely I could barely breathe. Not having the love of my parents ripped a gaping hole inside that I tried to fill with alcohol. And I swear, I thought my drinking was going to be temporary.

I thought what every addict in the history of addiction has ever thought: I thought all I needed was a little pick-me-up to get me through episodes with them—just this one last time, just until I get through these fucking holidays, just until I stop crying and then I swear, no more—and then I swear I will stop. Over and over, I told these lies to myself.

Twenty-five years later, I was so deep in my addiction to alcohol that I got sick and nearly died. I was sick for months before my body entered such a downward spiral of weakness that I had no choice but to get myself to a doctor. I was pale—jaundiced! Who knew Black people could get jaundiced? Not me! And yet, there I was becoming more sickly. I couldn't walk ten paces without running out of breath, sucking air like someone who just jogged a mile. My extremities, especially my fingertips, were always cold. I was wearing a scarf and gloves all day during my time at work. I was freezing in rooms that weren't at all cold.

Within ten minutes and a few questions about my drinking habits, the doctor I met with had me admitted to the hospital through its emergency room. I received a blood transfusion that very night. The next day, a nurse came into my room with wide eyes, shaking her head and marveling. This nurse told me how lucky I was.

I didn't feel very lucky because my doctor told me in no uncertain terms if I don't stop drinking, I could die. After being hospitalized for a week, I returned home. My husband had gone back to work and our children had returned to their own lives in neighboring cities. Once I was safely alone, I bawled and sobbed and keened until I thought I would faint from dehydration. I was terrified because I desperately wanted to live—I wanted to have gray hair, wanted wrinkled skin, and I wanted to see my children fall in love, partner up, and have their own children. But I didn't think I possessed the strength and determination to stop drinking. The longest I'd ever gone without drinking up to that time was nine days. I'd never been so scared of dying until the days after leaving the hospital.

I had to go back to the clinic for bloodwork routinely for several months. Just when my blood levels were going back up, just when I was beginning to feel healthy again, I gave in to the cravings that were by now riddling my body. I drank again. The blood levels dipped. My doctor called. I turned to a substance abuse program for help.

When I first joined AA, I was mortified to be there. Hell, these people were drunks and winos! How far I'd fallen, I remember thinking. Oh, the fucking shame of it. I didn't know yet that those thoughts were part of my addiction sickness. I was completely clueless that I was an addict. I was also distrustful of the overt friendliness of the members and the frequent entreaties for me to keep coming back. However, it wasn't long before I became excited about attending the meetings. It was the first time I'd ever been in relationships where so many seemed eager in being painfully honest, ALL THE TIME. Every meeting was about baring your guts and your entire soul (for those who chose to share). Some people would come primarily to listen, which was also good because when you're an alcoholic in AA, you attend meetings to help you stay sober. It's extremely helpful to hear addiction stories you can identify with because people are not generally sharing stories about their losing battles with addiction in the outside world. Listening to the stories is validating and it gives addicts like us hope. As someone who had felt the burden of secret-carrying for much of her life up to that point, the stories were a welcome relief. AA meetings literally saved my life.

I was a mess though. Getting sober was a process. It takes time, patience, and the humility to allow others to help you. This was one of the hardest parts for me. I had survived an abusive father and neglectful mother by my own wits. I had raised two children on my own. I had careers, held down jobs, paid bills, and helped keep the roof over my family's heads. I was accustomed to getting life done on my own. Yes, I was married. But the way I saw it, we were a partnership. I'd never ceded to helplessness in my life. I was a survivor. Unfortunately, due to all that independence, there were times when I thought I knew more than I actually knew.

I remember a meeting I sat in after being in AA for a year. I was sleeping better than I'd slept in years. My brain was clearing up. I felt sharper in thinking and my memory was beginning to work for me more often. I thought I was the shit, soberly speaking. So what if there were veterans of the program with ten, twenty, and thirty years of sobriety under their belt? I had an entire year under my bra-strap. There were newbies with way less time than me who were still jittery, still white-knuckling, trying to hang on and not go back to drinking. I was an old-timer—a veteran member of the AA program—now.

Phfft! I really wasn't. Not yet.

There I was one day, sitting in a meeting listening to someone talk about sobriety and how *time takes time* (a phrase AA old-timers use a lot and, as an impatient newcomer, I hated) and that person said this: it took five years of being sober for me to get my brain back.

I was incredulous! Five years? I can remember thinking, *well, that's because you're an idiot*. Because that math HAD to be wrong. How could someone need five entire years to be properly sober? That's just nuts.

Of course, I was missing the point of the speaker's message. I was missing the point because back then my brain was still swimming in alcoholic residue resulting from over-marinated brain cells, which swam in alcohol for more than twenty-five years. When I was still drinking, I had a skewed perspective on how I saw myself and how I saw the workings of the world.

If I was at work the next day after a night of drinking, I had to focus really hard to understand what I was reading in an email or a work document, sometimes rereading the damned thing six times over to get my brain to cooperate and absorb the information. A sober person who isn't distracted by wandering—boozy—thoughts can read a document once and understand it.

After spending years in the frontal lobe drunken dance, my thought processes, which were once slow-moving due to many tipsy/drunk/loopy days and nights, had to develop new habits of thinking. I had to retrain my brain into functioning on sober mode instead of on drunk mode. It would take practice.

So when I heard the AA old-timer talk about his mind still drying out from alcohol after five years of sobriety, my wayward brain got defensive—I didn't want to believe what he was saying because I was still thinking (even after a whole year of being sober) like an addict. No way did I want to admit this to myself. I didn't know yet how many sober days I would need to truly get my mind back, the mind that worked for me without the taint of drunkenness, the alcohol-free mind that I was born with.

That's not to say sobriety isn't just as important after three days as it is after thirty-three days or thirty-three months or thirty-three years. In AA, every single stage of sobriety offers crucial lessons its members can learn from. This is why we go to meetings because there's respectable wisdom to be gleaned at all stages of the sober journey from alcoholics willing to share their story.

As of this writing, I've been sober for ten years and four months. But drinking blotted away so much of my life.

I was forty-three when I stopped drinking. The only reason I stopped is because I got sick. I got so sick I had to be hospitalized for a blood transfusion to save my life. It was my bottom—the crash and burn event that can help an addict to get sober—and my wake-up call.

We didn't talk about addiction and alcoholism when I was a kid. Sure, I'd heard of it—this is your brain on drugs: an egg frying in a pan. But that was white noise to me, background chatter like birds chirping on tree limbs outside a window. That was a commercial and I was waiting for the show to come back on. We didn't talk about anything constructive in my household. Threats, demands, questions, answers. That was it.

I didn't know that alcoholism was in my future. All I saw was the possibility of getting out of my nightmare home alive and having the freedom to create my own life. There were no noticeable warnings about what drinking could do to me, what it could do to my future or what it could do to my health. Besides, I thought EVERYBODY drank. Beer and wine commercials seemed a constant backdrop for the American way. Happy hour beckoned. My friends and I responded. The world was large and overwhelming. My friends and I were about partying all the time. We thought we were the new guard, the new future. Like all the hippies and other youth who came before, we thought we would make the world a happier place. And all the drinking people just seemed so much nicer and more fun to be around.

Reality inevitably pressed in and caught up to us: rent had to be paid. My drinking buddies and I began to scatter, moving away from each other and into roles of full-fledged grownups. There were jobs, pregnancies, spouses and children to attend to. It didn't feel like it— as I was living through newly difficult seasons, almost totally unprepared for what was required of me as an adult—but life was zipping by as if someone had turned up the dial to make the rollercoaster go faster.

All of a sudden, it was me who appeared to be cranky all the time. I felt like a toddler whose juicy cup got snatched out of her hands, except my juicy cup contained vodka mixed with cranberry juice. *I was sober*. Not only was I sober, but sobriety also wasn't what I'd chosen for myself. I mean, yes, I chose it but only because I didn't want to die yet. I chose it because death was the alternative. I was forty-three. I still wanted to live. I still wanted to do things. But fuck me! I thought I would have more time with alcohol to figure it all out.

Apparently, most people interpreted my character as belonging to someone in an often-good mood when I was still drinking. I'd been giving off likable and agreeable vibes. But in my heart, I was full of rage and simmering with resentment. In my heart, I was screaming for blood. I was torn—as in, ripped to pieces underneath the rotating facades—in my differing roles of pretense, putting on and taking off masks to suit all the people-populated situations I had to navigate. The only person I could be my (almost entire) self with was my husband. But outside of him, I was always—*always!*—working at trying to be acceptable in the eyes of others. Without alcohol, I didn't know how to behave on my own. I didn't know how to be an ordinary person who wasn't wounded, ashamed, and in deep pain.

I was looking around at all the people, especially the ones I was trapped with during eight-hour workdays—I'd been working seven years in an all-white office—and I didn't think I could keep doing it. My crankiness turned to despair and I couldn't stop crying whenever I had a private moment. I was in agony. Something had to give.

I'd been writing all along—in journals, on blogs, and in unpublished manuscripts during my spare time. Although I never saw it as something I could ever do for a living—I began to seriously wonder about the dreams I once entertained as a young adolescent. A tiny dot of light was coming from someplace deeply buried in my mind. The more I wondered about who I was as a child with the dream to write, the brighter the light in my mind glowed. I began to peer into myself, seeking out the girl I once was, studying her in the mirror.

I realized, I'm still here. I didn't die.

Once ago, alcohol had been liquid courage, inspiring me to be braver than I felt in my heart, to do things I wouldn't ordinarily do in more sober moments. So when I got sober, I often felt deeply insecure about my abilities. One insecurity, in particular, I grappled with was thinking I was dumb. I spent my whole life pretending to be smart, but in my heart, I struggled to believe in my own intelligence. The soberer I got, the more I could see that I wasn't as dumb as I thought I was.

Sobriety has been reaping immense benefits, revealing the more resplendent sides of my own private world and the world we inhabit. I just needed to give my accruing sober days (time)—because *time*, does in fact, *take time*—to open my eyes and heart to a different outlook. That doesn't mean that the world isn't still full of pain, conflict, and chaos. But there's more to the world than the shit sandwiches it seems so full of. I needed sobriety to see that. Ours is a world of paradox: as splendid and life-giving as it is ugly and life-threatening.

I don't say all this to be preachy about drinking. The truth is, I had a blast when I was drinking. I wouldn't change all the fun and all the terrible days being an alcoholic brought. However, I needed to go back and figure out what happened, how I lost myself, how I crashed and burned only to rise again like a formerly broken warrior. I needed to tell the truth about my drinking in order to stop being so ashamed of that aspect of my life. The choice I made as a young adult to drink belonged to me alone. However, the fact is addiction is a disease. Addiction was never a choice for me.

I say all this because I've avoided long enough the fine details about what alcoholic addiction did to my life, how it set me back and how much time I lost because of it. All this avoidance—the way I tended to skim over my alcoholic story, not wanting to admit my loss of control and how helpless I was in the face of addiction—was keeping *shame* alive and strong in my heart.

These days I'm good with being an alcoholic. Especially if sharing my story helps someone else. My name is Mia and I am most definitely an alcoholic.

Thanks for sharing, Mia. Keep coming back.

You're safe here.

4

Turning My Blog Into A Book: Fail

Yeah, about that: the blog to book idea.

It should have been simple, really. At least that's what I thought when I decided to compile selections from my blog for a book. I'd written on that blog for well over two years, resulting in 119 essays—more than six hundred pages worth of writing. All I wanted was a small book to get my feet wet with writing and self-publishing before tackling the larger project of completing the manuscript for the Black women's friendship book. The research was done. Interviews had been transcribed, data was collated, and an unfinished manuscript awaited my renewed attention.

Transforming a collection of previously written essays from a blog into a book should have been... well, not exactly a breeze, but also not a doctoral dissertation on molecular biology either. I thought it was going to be easier than it turned out to be.

At first, as I began sifting through all the essays. They appeared decent enough for book reading. That right there, the feeling of the essays being *decent enough*, was my first hint that maybe this book was in trouble. I was trying to have this collection of essays published by Summer 2020 because I'd already announced it on social media. No way was I *not* going to have this (likely) smaller (less important) book done when most of my social media followers already knew that a larger (and more important) book project—also announced on the blog—had been previously in the works. So yes, I needed to get this book done.

I sent what I thought were the strongest essays—72 pages—to my book editor, Becky. I wasn't over-joyed with how the essays sounded. After they were published on the blog a few years ago, I barely looked at them again. I knew I should have revised the essays more before sending them, but in the weeks leading up to the date they were due to the editor, I was hit with all kinds of physical ailments, including getting the flu and having teeth issues, which required emergency dental visits. In retrospect, I'm sure my body was screaming at me to slow the hell down, but did I listen? Nope.

Becky completed the edits and gave encouraging feedback. When I got the edits back, I saw that the manuscript had gone from 72 pages to 63 pages (this meant my editor did some cutting). Ugh. It sucks when you know you could have done a better job of editing your own work. It sucks even more when a book editor confirms it. Privately, despite Becky's carefully worded, mostly positive feedback, I still wasn't feeling good about the essays. But I kept going because the next group of pages was about to be due.

Remember when I used the words *decent enough* to describe the blog essays? Heh. Yeah well, about that. The foreboding feeling I had was a prediction of coming disaster—fucking harbingers were everywhere. My body with its sudden illnesses, was screaming at me to stop. It was saying, please slow down and stop rushing this writing work.

When the next set of pages were due, I began having mystery pains in the joints of my shoulders and lower extremities. My anxiety spiked and I was feeling weepy. I've learned to respect crying and other emotional displays; they are the lighthouse which glows through the fog of overwhelm. As I began reading through the next set of blog essays to be edited, I wanted to scream and throw things. Most of them read like out-of-context excerpts, with endings that felt like unfinished thoughts. What might work on a blog doesn't always translate logically in a book.

Monkeywrench number one: many of the blog essays for round two of book editing sounded terrible!

It was time for me to admit this once and for all. There would *not* be a book of essays from a blog I once called *On Becoming Maria*. Why? Because the Maria who was writing on the blog in those early days—truth-telling and well-meaning, though she was—she was not much more than a jangle of nerves and broken pieces during those earlier blogging days.

That's the plain truth of the matter. I wasn't ready for book-writing, so I wrote on a blog.

I basically hit an inspiration block while trying to revise the essays. It was like being shaken awake, snapping to attention, and coming out of denial. The essays I'd been trying to rearrange to put into this book weren't going to work.

The blog had been an important tool on my book writing journey. I used my blog as a therapeutic outlet. It helped. The more I blogged at OBM, the braver I felt, and the more my confidence grew. But honestly? In my heart, I still felt like a loser most of the time. I was trying to write a Black women's friendship book and I realized—while blogging—that I was in way over my head. I couldn't shake the fear that seemed to consume every single breath, you know? I went to sleep with this fear. I woke up with this fear. The fear said, *you are a nobody and all the writing in the world will never change that.*

In my wounded heart I was still a girl, abused and hated in her original world of so-called family, and re-wounded again in the larger, more insidious world of an occasionally racist society.

I was a misfit. I didn't belong and I didn't fit in anywhere.

So what?

I challenged myself, pushing back. Why should you care about being a misfit? Focus on what's good. You have more—you overcame challenges, you acquired material provisions for both yourself and your family. You're already a kind of success story—than so many others who have so little. Work with what you've got.

My head is filled with mixed messages, what I know instinctively to be true (which is hard to follow with wavering self-belief) and what the world tells me should be possible. As a result, I'm often waging a battle inside myself, wrestling with basic choices, choices that may not seem as difficult to the next person. In the meantime, what has kept me going with writing is the knowledge that there are others in the world just like me. I met them during research for the friendship book: other women who also feel invisible, who also feel hurt and besides keeping their head down and working at their jobs and/or taking care of their families, aren't exactly sure what they should be doing in their lives to thrive and feel more fulfilled.

I carry the memory of those women in my heart. They remind me, this writing dream is the correct path, and to keep going and never give up.

Well shit, I'm trying. This is what *not* giving up looks like. This book of essays is happening, coming to you live as my writing life unfolds and hits the snags and bumps along the way.

There I was, sitting at my desk, staring at the computer, finally having arrived at the place of acceptance. Of one hundred and nineteen blog essays, I felt enthusiasm at the prospect of using merely five of them. That wasn't enough for the kind of book I had in mind for publishing. It might have been enough for a novella but not a full-size book.

Should I be telling you all this? Maybe not. Maybe you read this, roll your eyes, and toss this book aside, giving me a few brownie points for honesty since it saved you the trouble of possibly wasting your precious time. Telling you this is a chance I'm willing to take with the hope that it reaches at least one person like myself who's tired of seeing all the polished, finished products without the benefit of all the blood, sweat, and tears that built it. This is *my* kind of book, exactly the kind of book that gets me out of bed with the feeling that anything I put my mind to is indeed possible. I wrote it for me.

So now that I know I can't use most of my essays for the book I was hoping to publish by the end of Summer 2020, I do what I usually do in the face of overwhelm. I let the emotions wash over me and I cry like a baby. I turn off the phone, send necessary emails alerting all who need to know that I'll be out of touch, and I tell my editor there will be no more pages for the foreseeable future.

My body aches did not subside. I think, oh cool, maybe I'm dying. Maybe this is the end for me. It's what most middle-aged people think whenever inexplicable, random pain attacks our bodies. We fear the worst: bodies breaking down with age. I began thinking, looks like this is how I go out. Death is the best excuse for not finishing a book, so I might be in the clear.

However, just in case I wasn't dying, I went in search of a therapist and found one. Just in case I wasn't dying, I decided to take a couple of weeks off from writing because if I lived—obviously, my physical health did, in fact, return—I needed to give my mind room to get my muse and mojo back. I needed to allow for the mental calm that would bring inspiration to guide me towards writerly solutions.

Almost immediately upon meeting with my new therapist—through an online session due to the nationwide quarantine—the aches in my body completely disappeared. Call it stress-induced or psychosomatic—whatever it was, my body saved me from publishing the wrong book. I wanted a book that would inspire hope through tales of trials met and overcome.

It helped that my therapist was a Black woman. I'd never had a Black woman for a therapist in all the years I'd been in and out of therapy. In previous years, my therapists were white women. It was geography, basically. As an adult professional, I'd been fortunate to have a decent enough salary to live in middle-income neighborhoods, quiet areas with aesthetics, and extra land space between the homes. Those communities were located in suburban or rural areas populated mostly with white people. The downside is a lack of black professionals and service providers who'd likely have more insight and sensitivity to helping black families. The therapists' pool in these earlier seasons of my life were usually white. It never occurred to me that I might find a Black therapist if I tried online therapy. Being in quarantine left me with no other choice. That turned out to be the best thing to happen to me in a long time.

As a Black woman, being in therapy with another Black woman was like sitting down for wise heart-to-hearts with an older sister or a mother. This was huge for me. *Huge*. It would be the first time in my life that a Black woman in a position of authority stood up for me consistently. Here was a Black woman in my corner, telling me how great I am, how much I deserve happiness, and how I can win if I don't give up. Having girlfriends to gripe with about our respective heartbreaks is just not the same thing. Also, friends don't always know how to show up for you and cheer on an ongoing basis when life gives you wins. I learned this through my own experience and my research on Black women's friendships.

Black women tend to show mighty love to each other readily, especially in times of crisis. However, when things are calm in the life of our friends, we're usually working hard in our own separate lives, trying to meet obligations where we're most needed. As Black people, so many of us have had to overcome situations that were often the result of inequitable treatment and unequal access to resources. Too often, we've lived in circumstances behind the eight ball, struggling to come from behind. Friendships feel the weight of these burdens as they take their toll. We mean well, but we don't always remember to show up for each other consistently.

Talking weekly to a Black female therapist who always encouraged and offered kudos when I made good choices or had a successful moment was like having a cold drink after spending long hot days in the desert. It brought me back to life and it renewed my hope in what was possible for the future. We're Black, the therapist and me. The only awkwardness for us to get past was the newness typically present between strangers. There was no racial divide to tiptoe through, hoping to avoid landmines where offenses could delay access to inroads for therapeutic solutions. Getting past the newness as strangers was almost instantaneous because of our shared history.

I didn't have to be a mom, or a good friend, or a wife, or a super-woman of any kind. I could just show up to therapy as myself, show up as the unattached human I'd been as a younger person. And with this opportunity to think only about myself, I was able to reflect on the writing journey I'd been on in a new way. I was able to really lean in—without eyes on me, as they were when I blogged—and take a closer look at where I'd been and how life had impacted me at various turns.

I wrote down my findings, turning them into new essays for this book. Failing at the blog to book idea ended up being a blessing in disguise. It became a win-win for each of us, actually. New material for you, reader. And a needed emotional reckoning for me. History notwithstanding, how can any of us ever really know where we're going without understanding where we've been?

I'm not gonna lie, when I realized that I couldn't use all those blog essays that I'd counted on for a book, I thought I was screwed. But that near disaster became a neon sign flashing me towards a more inspired direction. And isn't that one of the beautiful surprises of life if we simply learn how to trust the journey and resist the urge to panic? Failures can turn into breakthroughs, and breakthroughs can become gifts.

Blog to book? A fail, yes.
But not entirely. Not exactly.

5

WE ARE ANGELS, WALKING ON EARTH
[*EXCERPT #1: OBM BLOG — MAY 2018*]

Note: When I was in my early forties, I started calling my mother *Lady* as a sort of endearment to her and a private joke to me. It had always felt awkward for us to relate to one another as grown women; we were more like strangers than mother and daughter, so *Lady* seemed a fitting name to call her. And she seemed to like it for reasons unknown to me. My parents are alive and living together—reunited a number of years after their divorce—in the same home I was raised in. We're estranged with no hard feelings between us. I love my parents despite all we went through together and I know they love me too in their own strained, klutzy way. After I got sober, I began talking about the childhood incest I'd experienced, telling the story out loud as a way to release the shame I'd carried about it for so many years. I told my story in therapy, in AA meetings, and in conversations with close friends. This was extremely difficult for me in the beginning because I'd kept it a secret for so long and I was mortified by the thought of people knowing. But the more I told the story, the less ashamed I felt about it. The first time I wrote about my sexual abuse on the blog, it appeared as the essay below.

* * *

Hey Lady,

After nearly two years of absence from each other's lives, it finally hit me that I may never see you alive again. Though it may seem unnatural, I feel like I've made peace with this revelation. Maybe I'd already made peace with losing you all those decades ago as we watched our paths diverge in one moment, a rare private juncture of whispered words between you and I. I bet you hoped I forgot. I bet you convinced yourself that you forgot as well. But I'm a mother now too, and experience has taught me that there are some words that pass between parent and child that can never be forgotten.

Why don't we just leave him?

Remember? I was eight when I spoke those words to you. In my naive thinking, sensing a moment of camaraderie between us, I thought maybe, if we just laid our cards on the table, if we simply spoke the truth of the matter out loud, maybe we could save each other. And it wasn't just watching him beat on you — that was the least of my worries. No, it was that days had bled into nights, weeks piled up until long months of my young life dragged into tortured years. I thought, surely an end had to be somewhere in sight. Mustering my little bit of temporary courage, I was pleading my case to you: *Mama, help me.*

Your swift, dismissive reaction told me all I did not want to know. Asking me if I was crazy, asking how would we live and how would we eat? The flash of anger in your eyes hinted at something else, a tell lost on an eight-year-old. All these years of feeling confused and invisible in the world, meanwhile, you were the one person who'd seen, saw with your more seasoned eyes something in me that scared you. But you never blinked. If you blanched, you hid it well, pretending to unsee what you saw. Troublemaker, right? Probably wondered how you could have birthed such a traitor, wholly disloyal to family bonds.

Eight years later—mayhem!

You were right. Our gravy train careened off the rails because I'd had enough and decided to draw a line into the fucking sand. Now I was sixteen and I could see the writing on the wall. Saving me was never in your cards. Papa was never going to stop. I had to save myself. Do you remember how sunny that Saturday morning was? I do. It was pretty outside, a warm summer day. But it was still early, so although the streets were sun-bathed, and fully leaved trees rustled gently, the block was quiet. I'm sure the neighbors must have ran to their windows when they glimpsed a police car, the rotating red and yellow lights flashing atop, and then — gasp! handcuffs? — isn't that the man who beats on his wife and kids?

By the time you got home from work, the street was quiet again, the tear stains had dried on my face, and your husband was sitting in a jail cell.

What did you do?! Your eyes were ablaze with fury.

Excuse me? Apparently, *I* was the culprit. I stared, searching your face, unprepared. Your reaction almost knocked me down. Your voice, Mama, those words sounded like an accusation. My heart raced. I felt trapped, felt so alone, nowhere to turn from your wrath and your bewildered rage. Your eyes were wild in defense of him. You flailed your arms, your eyes filled with tears.

Do you understand what you've done? In jail? You put him in there with murderers and rapists! How could you do that? How could you do such a thing?

You paced, you clutched your heart, shaking your head and ignoring my bewildered, angry pleas. You muttered words of comfort to yourself, saying, *Alright, think think think*!

That was some day huh, Lady? It was the day that changed us all, changed everything we thought we knew, brought alliances to the forefront, and fractured our family ties the way a stone cracks glass. Unfortunately for me, I was the stone.

Somehow our family managed to get through that season. You were always a clever one, Lady. You hid Papa in the basement, squirreled away his clothes and belongings from dutiful perusals by the social worker assigned to our home. I know you couldn't imagine allowing outsiders to help us. You two, a reprehensible team of fric and frac, left me no choice. We all paid dearly. Feels like we each made our own separate deals with the devil. Your deal, to pretend nothing awry ever happened, forced my own soul-crushing deal to zip my interloping lips for the foreseeable future.

Did I ever forgive you? You *know* I did. We moved on, despite our splintered family ties, kept up what you insisted on as needed appearances. You demanded and we followed, celebrating the mocking holidays, another Thanksgiving, another Christmas, another reunion for us all. Where did my rage go? Where did I store all those feelings of betrayal, all my grief? I was choking on the rancid pill of forgiveness, made harder to swallow in the absence of apologies or amends.

I wanted to be a good girl in your eyes for once, wanted to show you I had moved on. Besides, what good would it have done me to withhold forgiveness, Lady? We were already mere zombies walking, on auto-pilot often, moving stiffly through the mechanics of family life. Pretending to be okay. I stumbled blindly into the world, fairly clueless about my future life. Unforgiveness, I discovered, is a large and unwieldy weight of baggage to drag through an often cold and cruel world.

Despite your clear inability to parent—knowing your grandparenting attempts would be no better—I couldn't imagine blocking you from my kids. You seemed to love them in your own reluctant and angry way, but I had no manual for family dysfunction. I did what I thought was right, even if in my heart, it all felt wrong.

Finally, you went too far. Oh, there were little hurtful moments throughout our years—your micro-aggressions, the snide remarks, the little digs and insults, your "accidental" loss of things I cherished. Meh. I categorized these offenses as minor slights, seeing them for the pinches of pain they were, seven hundred and fifty-nine paper cuts to my psyche. I would live. Thankfully, we age because I must have begun to feel tired of you at last. When you created such a bad scene at your own granddaughter's college graduation, I knew I'd had enough of all our years of pretense. That hissy fit you threw? A tantrum because your abusive ex-husband had the audacity to bring his new wife to our celebration. That was the last straw.

Do you ever reread my letter? Or does it remain hidden at the back of some private drawer? Or did you simply throw it in the trash? Maybe you reflect with some regret on rainy or snowy days, when you're physically restricted, feeling lonely and nostalgic. Maybe you tell yourself an apology might not be the worst thing in the world. Do you? But then again, maybe you say, dammit! That would mean acknowledging everything we went through. And you refuse because, according to you, we should leave the past in the past.

Here's the thing, Lady. I know you thought that keeping our past buried was the best decision for us all. But the truth is, it was the best thing for *you*. You chose to keep your deal with the devil. As for me? I reneged and saw my life exponentially bloom. I told all our awful secrets, Mama. It surprised me—once the grief period had passed—how good I could truly feel. I felt lighter. I felt more loved. For the first time, I was full of hope for a life that could be lived with actual joy and gratitude. It's the wonder of self-love, Lady. I hope you get to experience it one day.

Thank you, Mama, you taught me things you probably never expected you'd be able to teach. I hope you find your own peace, if not in this life, then surely in the next. I think when we eventually meet each other on the other side, we'll fall into each other's arms and hug with the relief of long-lost sisters, reunited. Because I believe that we are angels with specific assignments here on this earth, and when we're done, we return to our angel life, having done what we were sent here to do. I love you, Lady, and I have no doubt you love me too.

Who's to say exactly how our connection as mother and daughter should meet its worldly end? It isn't for others to understand, as long as *we* do. I'm better, Lady. And I hope you're better too.

6

GETTING OVER APOLOGETIC BEHAVIOR

apologetic: 1. containing an apology
or excuse for a fault, failure, insult,
injury, etc. 2. defending by speech or
writing. 3. willing or eager to
apologize. 4. sorry; regretful.

I've lived an apologetic life.

Obviously, there's more to my personality than being apologetic. Among other things, I can also be thoughtful, snotty, hateful, pragmatic, and generous. But my apologetic tendencies became problematic in my early attempts to write a book.

The word unapologetic, although it's been a part of the English language for ages, seems to be a staple in millennial-speak. As far as I can tell, being *unapologetic* is a part of the millennial lexicon in a way that it just wasn't for us older people. I didn't know I was apologetic until I began listening to my own millennial offspring speak with admiration about artists and leaders of their generation speaking and behaving *unapologetically*. When I was a young adult, I never once heard any of our favored artists—singers, performers, writers—or leaders described this way.

Unapologetic? My interest was privately piqued. When I first began noticing the word *unapologetic* flying around—not just at home, but also on the internet, in books, and on television—I didn't want to admit to anyone that not only did I *not* know what they were talking about, but also, that it sounded—severely!—like the exact opposite of the kind of person I was at the time. I knew what apology meant. But I hadn't realized I was living in the constant act thereof.

And yet, if I wasn't being unapologetic, then ... well, shit.

It was like I was being followed through life by invisible mean girls. So annoying! How did they keep finding me? How do they seem to unearth my secrets before I do?

Because the truth is, when I took a closer look, I did actually notice the apologetic tendencies in myself. I'm not proud about admitting this, but the facts are the facts.

Here's what I also know to be true about myself as a writer. Among other things, I'm intelligent, wise, and imaginative. I can be humble, honest, and forthright. I try my best to shoot straight without holding back. I try to be respectful of individuals whom I care about. I love life and most of the humans on the planet tremendously and with my whole heart. Did I always believe these things about myself? Nope. I didn't. After job-quitting, I had to get to know myself, get to know what kind of woman I really was after so many years in different seasons of chaos.

For a long time, I thought I was a kind of loser, a social reject. I hated myself and the skin I was in. Sure, I knew I possessed some good qualities. My displays of confidence was self-taught and fledgling. Otherwise, who'd have ever hired me in my professional heyday? I was hiding in plain sight though, acting *as if* as a way to secure employment and get the job done. I didn't believe I actually possessed all the proficient qualities which earlier employers and colleagues saw in me.

When I quit the day job, I had to take stock of who I really was. I had to do an inventory of myself, admitting honestly what flaws and strengths there were. I had to tell myself the truth. I'm talking here about being apologetic because this character trait became a fly in the ointment of my writing life. I had no idea it was even a thing, being apologetic and having it interfere with one's work. To my knowledge, based on past experiences, apology fell in the verb category. You do something wrong or hurt someone's feelings, you apologize. That's it. But in 2020 the word apology became more of an adjective than it ever was.

I've talked about my sexually abusive childhood before. There was also rampant violence in my childhood home. My father used to draw courage from his drunken state, beating my mother and beating us kids whenever he got angry—which was often.

There are conflicting messages about how the members of the culture ought to treat their past in today's world. Most of the offerings suggest we should leave the past in the past and just "get on with it" or "get over it." The messages have been strong: suck it up, everyone has problems, put on your big-girl panties. I loathed these messages. Because for those of us who were once helpless children, it can be perplexing to move forward in this world, especially with its continued pronounced hostilities towards women and towards people of color.

The consequence of growing up in a home with violence and sexual abuse was becoming someone riddled with unworthy feelings. When you feel unworthy—because no adult in my young life was countering this internalized belief with anything hopeful or positive—you tend to feel like you should be sorry you're alive and getting in the way. Thus, my (unintended) frequently apologetic demeanor.

And with apologetic tendencies, I tried to do what I thought was expected of me as an adult: tried to properly fit in, hiding my not-normalness. I was desperate to blend in because I never felt like I belonged anywhere. I tried to heed the culture's messages about keeping eyes forward most of my life (decades!). Until at last, I realized it makes no sense. It makes no sense because we're not fragments of lives lived, we are entire beings. And we can't be true to ourselves if we're busy trying to prove that we're sucking it up and getting on with it like everyone should.

Not only did my father beat us during his foul moods, but my mother became a beater herself, taking a belt to our bodies over small infractions typical of children. My parents' beatings were less about the offensive behavior and more about getting us to submit to their power over us as kids. I know this because I went on—with less violence and on less frequent occasions—to do the same thing to my own children. Again, I am not proud of this. Cyclical abuse can happen. It was all about power and ego, reminding children of who holds the power. Whenever a sibling or I was getting punished with the belt, we cried the same refrain: yes, mama! or yes, papa! It was our cry to get the beater to stop beating us. It was the cry to indicate our understanding of the offense and the urgent promise that we would *never* let it happen again. It was the cry of **apology**.

I had no idea that this feeling—a desperate need to be seen as regretful, sorry, or apologetic—would stay with me and become a shadow over so many of my actions, as well as spoken and written words. Even when I came of adult age, acquiring the realization that my parents were wrong, likely battling mental illness during those awful years, I still had to deal with what the abuse suffered at their hands had done to me psychologically. Therapy was helpful, but it wasn't a cure-all.

Life is tricky for the formerly abused child. For most of adulthood, your greatest desire is to fit in. And your second greatest desire is to run away, leaving the past behind you … for good (you hope). Eventually, you realize—through movies, books, and talking with other people—that the past *always* catches up with you. You realize that you can never truly escape your past.

I kept running because I thought running was the only sensible way to fit in.

I didn't see right away how I was apologetic. I thought I was just super-nice when I liked someone. I thought I was just extra-kind and generous in my favored relationships. I ignored the rage and indignation that bubbled beneath my smiling face and simmered in my heart. I was trying to concentrate on being liked and fitting in. Especially in settings where my skin color made me the minority. I wanted to look like the anti-stereotype of Blackness (of course, nowadays, I give zero fucks about how non-Black people perceive me. Between the aging process and racial tyranny in America, I'm too tired for pretenses anymore). I wanted to look like a woman who wasn't angry. I wanted to look like a woman who was easy to get along with. I wanted to have the kind of love—even if it was collective, a little bit from each person I met along life's way—I missed out on getting from my parents. Boy oh boy, was I screwed. Because looking for the world outside myself to love me was like jumping out of the frying pan and into the flames.

There were also my personal relationships with loved ones among family and friends. I had to learn to stop behaving apologetic towards those I'd offended or hurt during seasons when I didn't know any better. Once I apologized for whatever bad behavior occurred on my part, I had to learn to let it go and move forward. I had to stop self-deprecating and shrinking myself constantly as a show of amends. In relationships, I came to realize how unhealthy it was to attempt living in constant apology as a way of making up for the bygone days when I'd fallen short. And shrinking myself was never going to make anyone feel bigger in their own life. I had to become my best self, the most authentic version, regardless of any past mistakes. I had to stop groveling for acceptance and simply begin trying to live a happier life, a life I could be proud of.

I learned a lot of lessons the hard—and sometimes re-traumatizing—way. In this way, I've been in good company with the majority of the adult populace. I've drawn needed wisdom where I could. Some of life's lessons are still a riddle to me. Apparently, this has been life in general for many other human beings, so I've often thought, no big deal.

However, not so with writing. It's quite a big deal to have the apologetic overtone in the words of a book. It sounds awful.

Members of an oppressed group can sometimes come off sounding apologetic. Women who say sorry to each other and other people every ten minutes over the smallest occurrences, even in situations where absolutely no apology is needed. My husband and I caught ourselves apologizing to each other excessively in the first half of our married life. We had to work hard to catch ourselves and stop it. Recently, I was on a phone call being helped by a customer service representative who I could tell was a young Black woman, likely near my daughters' ages. On the phone call, the service rep kept apologizing to me because she said her computer was repeatedly freezing. I told her that's okay once, but still, she wouldn't stop apologizing during our brief time on the phone.

When I first began writing the manuscript for the Black women's friendship book, I had stepped away from it for a few weeks to continue with some of the research components. When I picked it up again to return to writing, I reread the first few chapters. I hated all those pages so much I trashed them and started over. I was shocked and frustrated with the overly apologetic tone in my writing. I thought I wasn't worthy enough to write a book about social issues in those earlier book writing days. Back then I still thought I needed someone's permission to speak about issues impacting Black women. I was still a work in progress, still learning how to believe in myself, still learning to internalize the feeling of belonging to my own experiences, and still learning to accept that I deserved to do and be whatever I wanted in this world, including writing a book about Black women.

Black people are not monolithic. We come bearing a wide variety of perspectives, appearances, belief systems, languages, and experiences. We need way more books about us than there is currently available to read. While there've been hundreds—likely thousands! —of excellent and entertaining books written by talented and eloquent Black writers, we continue to be in dire need of even more books written for us and by us, which might attract additional Black people from broader Black experiences that continue to be underrepresented. We need all the help we can get to advance us, which means numerous channels for a broader spectrum of resources. We can't afford to restrict ourselves with the kind of limited thinking that suggests only a select few among us can lead or teach or guide. We should be encouraging each other to have all hands on deck. Every single one of us has something unique and worthy in our lives to contribute.

Not everyone is into reading novels or science fiction or romance or political or social commentary. Not everyone is into reading memoirs either. But the thought of attracting readers who may have searched and come up empty looking for a book like this one makes me happy. We need as much diversity in our books as we can make available to each other. Especially in light of the traumatizing and painful times we Blacks have been experiencing in America lately (police murdering unarmed Black women and Black men). I've read a number of outstanding books about our historical plight as Black people by some of the most brilliant political, cultural, and scientific Black thinkers of our time. And while those books have been helpful to those who actually took time out to enlighten themselves by reading, there are still large numbers of Blacks who will never read those kinds of books.

So I had to stop sounding apologetic in my verse because I actually *do* belong to something important, whether I believe it entirely or not, whether it intimidates me or not. I belong to the experience of Black pain. Not all of us can be celebrities such as athletic stars, musical artists, media moguls, movie actors, etc. Just because we see more Black celebrities among us in recent years doesn't mean that the challenges and difficulties typically faced by Black people are issues of the past. An inordinately large number of us are still struggling, still suffering, and still feeling the sting of our wounds. Some of us are estranged from family members and estranged from friends who were once dear to us. Some of us are without a network of support around us, leaving a few (or much more) feeling vulnerable and lonely in a world that is more often than not hostile to people of brown and black skin. Some of us struggle with addiction to substances or are connected to a loved one battling their own addiction. We hurt. But we live in a world that has trained us to stay buttoned up about our pain, including the world of our own smaller communities and families.

The more we begin finding ways to open up about our pain—be it through memoirs, social media, documentaries, or other media—the more we'll be able to see that others are going through exactly what we're going through, that we're not the only ones trying to get through a painful season.

I'm learning how to stop feeling apologetic about who I am in the world. As I get into the practice of rebuffing apologetic behavior, as I stop feeling embarrassed about the life I was given, and as I find the courage to be braver about showing my personal battle scars to the world, I hope another Black woman (or any person) can draw inspiration from these pages and share her own story with someone else who needs it.

7

DREAM-CHASING CAN CRUSH YOU UNDERFOOT

Almost immediately upon entering adulthood, I fell into survival mode when it came to my finances. Before I even walked to the thrilling tunes of college graduation ceremony music, I already had credit card debt. I barely knew what good or bad credit meant, but I had a steadily growing amount of debt.

My parents were homeowners and I had no idea what that meant. As a twenty-two-year-old, I vaguely understood what a mortgage payment entailed. I knew about paying rent. I'd had a studio apartment during my senior year of college. The apartment had a few pieces of furniture: a couch with a pull-out bed, a table, and two chairs. I had some dishes and flatware. I worked part-time in a nursing home, making just enough to pay the rent and continue attending classes full-time (this was thirty plus years ago, rent was cheaper back then). I was attending a state school; tuition was paid largely by government grants and student loans. So, in addition to the two credit cards (of the predatory kind with high interest on a mere few hundred dollars for the beginning balance), I was graduating college with student loans that would follow me well into my thirties as a working professional.

How did this work exactly? The loans and their interest. The credit cards and *their* interest. Monthly payments. I understood none of it. I didn't study the monthly statements when they came. Sometimes I didn't even open the envelope because there'd been months of skipped payments in my wake. Whenever I did pay, I paid only the minimum required amount. I was digging a hole into bad credit which would take years to climb out of.

How would I have known these things? How does one acquire such information while trying to survive their childhood? I snatched information in pieces through public school, television, novels, and friends. What I managed to piece together, I merged with the learn-as-you-go action that was unfolding in my life.

Nowadays, I'm smarter and my credit is practically stellar. But I had to learn about personal financial management the really hard way. I had to fail miserably first.

I suppose this is the reason why taking such a risk as quitting my job of seven years—abruptly deciding in middle-age that I wanted more out of life before I died— to pursue writing dreams didn't properly frighten me as it should have. I'm not a newcomer to risk-taking. I've flown by the seat of my pants in various seasons of earlier years because I had no choice. In the earlier adult periods of my life, situations tended to be sink or swim. I know what it is to come from behind—like so many other Black people accustomed to making a way out of nothing when jobs and other resources are typically inequitable and, therefore, hard to come by—with money, patiently building funds back up from zero.

However.

Dream-chasing in middle-age has been the hardest thing I've ever attempted. I'm elated that I stuck with it and found my footing along the book-writing journey. I really am happy to be here, doing this. At this point, it's no longer about the money, as in becoming someone else's definition of success. It's not about being rich and famous. However, money-making is certainly not off the table of my desires. I'll take it when it comes, that's for sure. But the fact is, I've arrived. I'm already living the dream I imagined for myself. I'm working every day, doing the one thing that I've always enjoyed doing.

That is one aspect of my reality, being happy with writing full-time, even while there isn't yet any money in it. I do this work because it gives me life; it makes me thrive. And yet, there's also another aspect of my reality which is this: if I'd been shown the future of what dream-chasing from the margins in middle-age was going to look like, I would have stayed put in a job that was increasingly sucking the life out of me and making me utterly miserable. I would *never* have quit had I seen this future.

Crazy right?

Maybe I've confused you. On one hand, I hated my job, so I quit. Now I'm thriving, living my best life. Even though there's no money in it (yet!), I get to do what I love, which is writing full-time. But on the other hand, it also sounds like I'm saying, if I'd known specifics of the difficulties ahead in pursuit of dreams, I would have stayed in the job which was making me miserable?

Yes, it's a completely paradoxical truth.

The bottom line though is, I wouldn't change a thing about what I've learned so far. I would keep everything about my life today exactly the same. In other words, I wouldn't want a do-over. Because the fact is, there is no crystal ball, so there isn't any way to see into our future. Hypotheticals are just thoughts. I'm merely saying, thank god I didn't know how tough life was going to get after quitting the job.

Yes, dream-chasing has been hard—I mean really *fucking hard!* —but it's also been rewarding.

The reason I say I wouldn't have quit my day job if I could've seen the future is because if I knew that I was going to have to walk through what has at times felt like a raging fire, to get to the other side, knowing I would get burned, I would've been too terrified to try it. But I did it. And I've learned a lot!

When I first quit the job, I was thrilled: cheesing every day, grinning like an idiot, I swear. It felt like I was frequently on the edge of hysterical laughter, like in my mind, I was playing the funniest joke ever told on loop in changing, goofy voices. It felt like I escaped a near-death experience, like I'd cheated it, like I'd been sentenced to die, but had managed to somehow crawl through a secret hole towards freedom and made my getaway.

Those giddy feelings lasted a few months.

Once they were gone, after gradually fading away, Fear moved back in. And from that moment on—even up to this very minute as I write—my moods have swung like a wild pendulum through the emotional spectrum which exists between *fear* and *courage*. In the beginning, when these emotional swings were happening, it freaked me out, and I'd often find myself stuck for extended periods in panic mode. I wondered if I fucked up by quitting, wondered if it was too late to get my old job back.

After a while, I realized this is normal. It comes with making major life-changes. And I'd shake it off and keep working. But it wasn't easy, it took some getting used to. It took practice.

Another thing I didn't anticipate? Loneliness.

Lonely feelings would creep up and possess me, spreading over my body like a fever. Ugh! All of a sudden, I was missing *everybody*, no matter what role they ever played in my life.

During the last year before I quit, Howard (my awesome husband) helped me remodel our junk room, turning it into a home office. The colors I chose for decorating had a pink and yellow theme. I'd never had my own bedroom in childhood, and we weren't given the extras typically given to well-loved children for decorating. The childhood bedroom I shared with my younger sister was strictly functional, furnishings for basic needs only. The bedroom walls were painted white, like all the other rooms in that nightmare house.

Howard had painted the walls a soft yellow and spray-painted an old file cabinet my chosen cotton-candy pink shade. Once I'd finished clearing out all the junk from the room and filling the space with office furnishing and decorative items, my home office became a second chance, a princess-like space to call my own for the first time. I loved it!

When my work-from-home days commenced, and Howard left for work, I found myself alone in an empty house, feeling less and less excited. Our nest was empty; the kids had grown up and were living in their own separate apartments. At first, I couldn't wait to be alone. But once I got the added freedom I'd wanted for so long, it felt weird. It was an adjustment. I no longer had the obligations—constantly cooking, trying to keep the menu varied and tasty, taking care of everyone—of motherhood. I didn't have to go into a workplace and spend long hours with co-workers. When I was still working I used to hide out in my office most of the time, avoiding office banter, which usually required performance from me, pretending to be interested in unrelatable topics of conversation. And yet, at home, on my own, I was unprepared to feel so all alone. Everyone was gone and the silence in the absence of other bodies suddenly felt more pronounced.

I had to learn how to get through the lonely feelings. There was a period of acclimating. As a cure for the shock of loneliness in the initial months, I did my writing work in coffee shops, at the library, and mall food courts. I did this until I found a rhythm that worked for me. Nowadays, I'm back to preferring to spend most of my writing hours alone, in the comfort of home. I usually write at the pink desk (an online find at Ikea) in my office, on my bed with a laptop (like I'm doing now), or on the couch in the living room.

But holy crap, I had no idea that lonely feelings could be so nearly crippling to the stay-at-home working life.

The fact is, no one really tells you these things about dream pursuits and trying to make a better life than the one you may have found yourself living. Oh yeah, sure, there are some books about cautionary tales, maybe some self-help kinds, and yes, even the underdog stories. Yet and still, I've read hundreds of books, and I've only ever lucked up and stumble on a handful of the nitty-gritty (sans the graphic details about trauma), no-holds-barred kinds of truth-telling in books. I've already seen all the shiny, cleaned up, and bedazzled versions of story-telling that I care for at this point as a woman in her fifties. Now I'm ready for some non-mainstream types of reading material. Not porno or erotica, exactly, but something in that ballpark. Something more brave and less precedented. I need egg-on-face, oozing down, kind of vulnerability in my content. Because that's what dream-chasing looks like.

But before I go deeper with my own nitty-gritty, vulnerable happenings, I need to explain my crash-course lessons-learned with relationships in the wake of a reinvented lifestyle.

I'm no multi-album selling singer, but there's a song British vocalist Adele sings which resonated with me right away when I first listened: *A Million Years Ago*.

Deep down I must have always known

That this would be inevitable
To earn my stripes I'd have to pay
And bear my soul
...
When I walk around all of the streets
Where I grew up and found my feet
They can't look me in the eye
It's like they're scared of me

The lyrics are about how much she's changed and how different things are now with the people she used to know. I was forty-nine and I'd already begun to question who I'd become. I was already yearning for something more, leaning towards the pull of something I couldn't explain. I was changing. There were moments when I'd be in conversations—listening to the voices, watching lips move, staring at mouths opening and closing—but sometimes it felt like I was hearing the talkers from a distance, like sitting at the bottom of a pool, ears full of water, while they talked from above.

You know that feeling? It's like you're there, but you're inside your thoughts more often than you're in your body, having a conversation with whomever. It's surreal; life is unfolding with you in it but you're on the outside of yourself, watching. Right. So I was already gone from most of the people who knew me before I ever actually left. I'd been making plans, making changes.

There's no manual on how to keep growing into the person you want to become while maintaining relationships with friends and family.

When I attended AA meetings, I would listen to stories about how loved ones sometimes resented the changes in a newly sober person, how they didn't always know how to deal with them being so different in sobriety versus how they were as drinkers having a good time.

But what about becoming a dream-chaser? Would all the dream-chasers raise their hands so we can discuss? In society, we're well-trained in talking with each other about the familiar things like going to jobs (even if most of us hate our jobs), living for Fridays, hating Mondays, and taking vacations. But if you decide to become an entrepreneur or an artist or chase a dream, while most people around you continue with life as everyone knows it in the daily grind, conversations between you and them tend to feel less fluid. Birds might even chirp while we do quick mental searches on what to ask each other at family gatherings or holiday meet-ups.

Which brings me to the next unexpected ripple in the splash of mid-life changing—*feelings of paranoia*.

When you're spending the day doing work life completely different—*wait, so all you do is sit at the computer and just write? But what <u>else</u> do you do? —* than the average working person, it can feel like you're the only one living this kind of life. Yes, absolutely, there are other work-from-home people on the planet. And certainly, other artists are pursuing their passions full-time. But workers like us appear in fewer numbers than ubiquitous nine-to-fivers.

Since I'm the only full-time writer I know at the moment, during downtime, whenever I'm not writing, my mind has tended to occasionally wander. Our minds can get bored, and the voices in our thinking can be mercilessly mean and mischievous.

I start to think that I'm being perceived as some kind of vagrant weirdo and maybe people are discussing this about me. They're not. But my mischievous mind likes me to think that they are.

And then my rational mind says, cut it out, no one is talking about you. The more time I've spent alone, the more I think I understand why Kanye is the way he is. Paranoia is really a thing.

Obviously, I've learned to reign my thoughts back in. But it's an on-going practice, let me tell you. I had to develop some tricks to redirect my own thoughts, like flashing something shiny in front of a crying infant as a distraction. I know! Grownups shouldn't still need to apply such tactics. But trust me, we never really stop being the little people we once were.

My tricks included taking walks for fresh air and a change of scenery. Sometimes I'd play loud music and dance. Sometimes I'd crochet while re-watching a favorite movie. Stuffing my face with sweets is another favored distraction.

Being your own boss takes dedication and commitment. All I knew about working from home were the romantic aspects. I thought I would take a bunch of naps, some long lunches, and dive into random Netflix rabbit holes. While I did, in fact, do all of those things in the beginning, the process of book writing was absolutely unsustainable under the same tent as those slacker habits.

And while we're on the subject of breaking habits, I also had to learn how to be okay with the unpredictable nature of the writing process. The *unknown* became a place that I needed to get comfortable existing in. With day jobs, predictability is our bread and butter. We know to expect a paycheck every two weeks. We show up when we're supposed to, at the same time every morning (or night). We usually take our lunch breaks around the same time and we also usually eat the same kinds of lunches. Seasons rotate, bringing with each the usual variety of chatter about whatever is trending that week (of all the routines of the workplace, I hated these routine conversations the most): Oh man, looks like snow (no shit, it *is* January in the mountains) or Did you buy your turkey yet? You start your Christmas shopping yet? Ugh. So much about the world's daily grind has tended to be predictable and most of us have liked things this way. Even me.

However, most of the predictability disappeared when I quit the job. I had to pivot in a hurry. There'd be very few predictable moments to nestle in as someone who was now working for herself. That meant a loss of control most of us are accustomed to having. I'd spent several decades living in the comfort zone of the predictable. Once I quit work, almost everything in the foreseeable future became unknown to me. That was *so* not easy.

It's doable, though. You learn how to manage.

Finally—and to me, this is the suckiest part about being an artist/writer—I had to be okay with failing, and not just failing but failing spectacularly.

This is the one thing that all of the artist/business/entrepreneur books *do* warn you about. But when I used to read those passages, I convinced myself that maybe it won't happen to me. Or maybe if it has to happen to me, it won't be so bad, it'll be some kind of gentle failing, the kind no one notices.

When I read that this would happen, my mind instantly rejected it. It's like reading a book about experiencing labor pains while you're still in the second trimester of pregnancy. Oh yeah, the pain is explained and yes, it does appear that possible sobbing and ripping flesh may be a part of the inevitable labor experience. But the mind goes into protection and self-preservation mode, rebuffing such body-traumatizing predictions. You know there's no going back now—since you are very pregnant, indeed—but you need reassurances in order to go forward, so you lie to yourself, with the hope that your labor will be different, that what's being described is a mere exaggeration and you could possibly be the one in a million exception to the rule. Yes!

But, sadly, no.

My mind just would not compute: huge failure? Nah. It won't be that bad. I doubt it will be that bad. Even though there are plenty of examples all around us every day of artists who bombed in public performances and kept pursuing their dream anyway. And just as many examples of businesses that go belly-up before the entrepreneur figured out her mistakes and tried again, eventually finding success. Inventors who invent clap-trap clunkers before inventing something so germane to our lives, they went on to become millionaires.

Still, despite of all the evidence, I didn't want to believe this, that I would fail.

Well, I failed. I tried podcasting and that was a dud (episode after episode, with practically no listening audience, until I finally took the hint and closed up shop at the end of two seasons). Then there was the blog, *On Becoming Maria*. I blogged transparently, logging my creative journey, finding a large audience only to freak out under the gaze of so many reading eyeballs, that I began writing (yapping) nonsensically until I lost many of the followers. I now understand what it feels like to fail spectacularly. At first—ugh! like a drop-kick into your chest cavity—it felt like the wind was knocked out of me. I was like, oomph! What just happened? I felt embarrassed. I thought maybe this creative life was a mistake. It wasn't. But I couldn't help but wonder.

I'm still here. I could very well be in the midst of another failing project with the writing of this book. There's no way for me to know in this moment. I just have to keep going until I'm done, keep going until my editor reads and gives the manuscript back for another round of edits, and keep going until I publish and it becomes a book. It's part of living in the *unknown*, the unpredictable nature of the artist's life. You never really know if you're failing or succeeding until you've gone all the way through it and are living on the other side, in the floodlights of hindsight.

It's a risk worth taking, made easier by the desire to write more for me than for anyone else. Are these *all* my lessons-learned? No way! Capturing all the lessons gleaned from dream-chasing would be like trying to capture everything I learned during four years of college or everything I learned as a parent who raised children to adulthood. I would need more books, like a series in an on-going story. The lessons learned in this book are merely my favorite ones on the journey so far.

I love writing. I love creating. I love sharing stories as an avenue towards inspiring other women (and men). Dream-chasing is hard, yes. But it's so totally worth the good feelings it brings. Dream-chasing isn't much different than ordinary life. There are highs and lows, sunny days and stormy days. With dream-chasing, I learned how to reconcile the gloriously wonderful happenings with the shit-staining horrendous occurrences. In other words, I learned how to fall down, get back up, brush off, and keep moving.

8

COURAGE NOT GUARANTEED
[*Excerpt #2: OBM Blog – May 2018*]

Note: In discussions about my work, my contemporaries were often surprised by my ability to walk up to complete strangers and just start talking to them, inviting them to take surveys and sit down with me for interviews. I saw how these contemporaries marveled. During those weeks of researching, I marveled at my own boldness too. But those good feelings of marvel happened only on the good days, and good days were rare in the early months.

For a brief period in my early twenties, I was a reporter whose press credentials gave her permission to walk into offices at the New York State Legislature Building, ask for interviews with politicians, and fully expected to be granted those interviews, either on the spot or within days.

Fast-forward thirty years. Now I'm a middle-aged blogger with no official authority, asking strangers for minutes of their time so that I can gather information for my very first book. It was one of the hardest things I'd ever tackled and I did it with my youthful days—when I had more energy, had the younger appearance approved of by society, and felt invincible—long behind me. It was like signing up to be a salesman. You go in knowing there may not be any sales in the beginning. You go in knowing you will get rejections. But no matter how well-armed you are with these facts, it still feels devastating whenever someone firmly tells you *no*. Because it's not always just a no. Sometimes it's a no delivered with rudeness or hostility. Yes, there's a difference between the two and they both feel awful. I wrote the essay below when I was nine months deep in research and writing the Black women's friendship book. I wrote it as a letter to myself, as a way to build myself up to keep going and not give up. I wrote it through tears. Tears were my constant companion on the writing journey. The tears became the lighthouse which led me home through frequent foggy nights.

* * *

Dear Lovely,

No one is coming to meet you. There is no special guide or savior. You are going to have to travel this creative path and put your whole heart further into it. You are going to have to meet yourself.

People like you aren't meant to make it because out here, the word on the streets is, it's *dog eat dog* and *only the strong survive*. You with your tender heart, your earnest gaze, and your occasionally sad, watery eyes. I know how you feel, Lovely. Sometimes it can appear daunting, tiny little you against the big, wide, crowded, and cynical world.

You are the one you've been waiting for. Wrap your head around that. The once brokenhearted among us— those who climbed out of their pain and their misery, those who figured out how to win, those who now stand near the top of life's pyramid as if all the broken glass they crawled across left no bloody trails—they've been expertly trained to stiffen their upper lip, sharpen their claws and preemptively strike wherever possible.

No one is coming to meet you. You are going to have to meet and help yourself.

You are standing at the precipice and it's time for you to decide, another corner to turn, another fork in the road, another dark tunnel to step into. I know, here it comes again. Fear. Panic. Terror. You'd like to think you can't, but it isn't so, you actually *can* … and you know you have to.

I know you thought you were done. You're in middle-age, for fuck's sake. How much more healing could there possibly be? You'd already taken stock— material possessions seemed accounted for, health appeared on the better side of fair. PTSD mortality? Still breathing, so yes, check. Sobriety? Check. Self-awareness? Check. Marriage strengthened? Check. Maternal improvements? Check. Your kids are safe? Check.

But wait, what's this? Courage and self-love not guaranteed? Nope. Reset button needs hitting daily

…. for-fucking-ever? Yes. I know, I'm sorry, life can be as complex as it is simple.

Go ahead, Lovely, cry it out. Tell them the truth about how hard this really is. There is no cap on broken-heartedness after you've survived life with *no parents* in your corner, after you've survived rapes, violence, and alcoholism. You *do not* have to suck anything up. You don't have to pretend that because you've reached a few pinnacles, that you're done feeling lost, that you're done feeling confused or done feeling vulnerable. You're allowed to cry as much as you need to.

Go ahead and cry. Let them know that feeling your feelings is the source of your super-power. Let the world see that a few imagined demons of Fear, Shame, and Rejection, all with their long, sharp teeth dripping slime, all with their claws raised— let the world see the way their power fades when you stand up to the ghosts and face them down. Let them see the brave girl in you who taught herself the art of surviving and thriving for all these decades.

You must keep showing up, Lovely. There are countless others out here just like you, battling their own Fear-Demons. There are way more numbers of you and others bearing bravely up against life's storms than there are gatekeepers trying to sustain outmoded ways of thinking and living. Sound the battle cry, let them see you and hear you. Stand and be counted. Show others how strong we all can be if we keep showing up with our hearts, proffering our love.

You haven't done anything to be ashamed of, Lovely. You were given this life and you're still living it. Cry it out. Let them see your tears. Let them see what it looks like to regenerate courage, getting up after you've fallen down, and pressing forward through spaces echoing with solitude. Sound your battle cry so more of us know how much we matter. Once ago, we were helpless children, now we are warriors of survival. Don't you ever hide, Lovely. You deserve the space you are standing in. Keep going. The World needs us.

You are stronger than you know.

I love you.

Sincerely,

Stronger Self

9

WRITING DURING A NATIONAL QUARANTINE

When I first began working on this book—when I still believed that most of it would be made up of essays from the blog—I thought there wouldn't be much new writing required of me. Not only had I never heard of COVID-19, but also the idea of being restricted to my home was as far off my radar as donning a spacesuit for a flight to the moon. As COVID-19 death tolls rose across American soil and a kind of stifled panic began to spread, the reality of what we were all experiencing in separate local areas began to take hold. It was a slow but quite deliberate dawning of understanding. We were in a national crisis.

I stopped reading COVID-19 news updates after the initial six weeks of quarantine as a way to keep focused on writing this book. When I say stopped, I mean I stopped googling news updates. We have no cable in our home. My husband and I are parents of three adult children, all who live elsewhere, leaving the two of us in an empty nest. Nowadays, we don't watch as much TV as we used to.

We have two working televisions which we use on infrequent occasions to watch DVD movies or live-streamed programming with a computer. I don't have a news outlet app or email app on my phone. I'm one of what seems to be a steadily shrinking pool of people who use their phone primarily to communicate with another live person. If I want to know what's happening in the news, I do an internet search on the computer. If I want to sift through the overwhelming deluge of emails often flooded with junk advertisements, I do so while on my computer.

All I really knew about the quarantine was what I saw on the occasions when I'd get into my car and drive to a store for groceries. I also got updates by talking with family and friends from other states during routine phone calls. At the time of this writing (Summer 2020), we're still living in quarantine, though less stringently so in our Pennsylvania area. Every store I go to now requires all customers to wear masks. I keep a mask in my car. I don't put the mask on until I am entering the store and I take it off as soon as I walk back outside of the store. I absolutely hate having to wear a face mask everywhere. I hate this new reality of living in a world where half of our faces are covered, creating a new distance between strangers that widens the previously tense chasm we'd already been experiencing in the still palpable wake of a presidential election—2016—which amplified political differences. It feels like we're even less friendly nowadays, wearing masks than we were before. I honestly didn't think we could get less friendly and more tense with each other as citizens. The quarantine has proven me wrong on that note.

The COVID-19 pandemic was my second major national crisis.

When 9/11 happened back in 2001, I was a single parent of school-age children, living in the New York City area. After a twelve-year absence, I'd been back to my Brooklyn hometown for a mere two years. It was a temporary move that was ending as I made the transition to our more permanent home in Pennsylvania. I'd been changing cities due to my financial struggles as a single parent every few years. Pennsylvania was about to be my last move for a long time. Although I'd left close friends behind in at least two of the cities I lived in before moving back to New York, I didn't have what you would call a real social circle around me any longer. When I wasn't traveling for work, my downtime was mostly spent taking care of my children. I was basically a loner during those two years living in New York besides the occasional meet-up for drinks and/or dinner with co-workers or other friends.

I had no experience with living through a national crisis such as 9/11. The family I'd created for myself was all I had: I was a divorced mother with two young daughters in grade school. The offices where I worked were a mere few blocks from where the towers had fallen, so our office building was shut down immediately following the terrorist attacks, and I was out of work for about a week.

I honestly didn't know what to do, so I watched the news every day for hours at a time. I wouldn't recommend this in a national crisis. It was very depressing. The initial search through the large debris of crumbled buildings moved quickly from a search for survivors to a search for recovered bodies and body parts. For weeks the news reports were packed with footage of ground zero recovery efforts and footage of live funerals for first responders. Our country was in the grips of the aftermath of a terrorist train wreck and I, like so many other Americans, had a hard time tearing ourselves away from the television to look away.

When we returned to work less than two weeks later, it was hard to focus. The first few days were given to tears and shared recollection of traumatizing 9/11 stories: where we were when the towers fell, who we knew that had died in the towers or on one of the planes used as a missile, how we got home that day, and how many hours it took us. Those of us who were at work when the buildings fell had to walk across the Brooklyn Bridge to get home while the dust and detritus from the explosion drifted through the air in large particles rivaling snowflakes. Those unlucky individuals got covered in deathly debris, grime, and gunk. Most arrived home covered in so much dust they looked like Halloween revelers painted in dirty chalk. I was one of the lucky ones.

I'd been at a New York airport that morning waiting to board a plane for business travel. But since all planes were immediately grounded, I was able to share a cab—there were too many of us in the airport to hail private taxis; the lines for getting a taxi were extremely long, causing significant wait times—back home. All in all, my usual thirty-minute car ride from the airport to home turned into a roughly two-and-a-half-hour journey due to multiple stops to drop off passengers. Since public transportation was also grounded, some of my co-workers spent as many as four hours walking to their respective homes on foot. Because for some, they lived at least an hour's train or bus ride away from their jobs in the city.

It would take a few weeks for work-life to resume anything resembling normal. We all rallied to get back into our work routines. After a few months of being glued to the evening news, I finally decided to stop tuning in. It was all largely morbid and not getting any better. I don't remember where this message came from, but I heard it more than once during those awful initial months of post-traumatic shock due to the terrorist attacks: Americans should get back to their lives, show the terrorists that we did not buckle and that we were not defeated by their heinous acts of destruction. But of course, not everyone was heeding this suggestion. For some of my co-workers, it was all they could think about and talk about. I began to avoid the watercooler.

I still had children to raise. I didn't have the luxury of being caught up in the country's panic or their outrage. So I tuned out. A few months later, we moved to Pennsylvania.

Almost two decades later our country is hit with a new national crisis: a pandemic outbreak of a virus called COVID-19. And I have the nerve to be writing a book.

There are unprecedented death tolls across the country numbering in the tens of thousands (over 240,000 by November 2020). People are terrified. The government is on high alert, issuing quarantine directives based on instructions issued from the Centers for Disease Control. Not that 9/11 wasn't devastating and traumatizing in the loss of lives. A childhood friend of my brother's, someone who grew up down the street from where we lived, lost his mother in the towers. For New Yorkers, each of us had a 9/11 story about loss that we could tell. Like I said, everyone knew someone who'd died in the attacks. But 9/11 seemed to suddenly pale in comparison to the tremendous body count— across the globe—from lost lives due to COVID-19.

This time around, during a national crisis involving the sudden death of tens of thousands, I have networks of people with whom I'm actively connected. This time around, during a national crisis, I'm married. My children are now adults with their own lives. Now, instead of being distanced by the fractured ties to toxic family members, I have loving in-laws in my life—even if most of them live hundreds of miles away from us in different states. Now, I also have friends with whom I keep in touch in neighboring states.

For a while, at the beginning of the quarantine, I'm connecting with loved ones almost daily. We're keeping each other apprised of developing news. But I can't get my bearings enough to keep going with book writing. Once again, as I live through a national crisis, I find I have no idea what to do. None. When we get on the phone the conversations I'm having with loved ones are merely stunned updates to each other.

I'd just begun to assemble the essays for this book before the quarantine was declared for our area. It was mid-March 2020 and pages had been written and sent to my book editor. I was in the midst of combing through old blog essays, mining for more content to include in the book. I had a deadline to meet—though I was the one who set it, so it could be changed at any time—to deliver the rest of the pages to my editor.

I was often on the phone with loved ones as a sort of checking-in, making sure everyone was okay. Thankfully, everyone we—Howard and I—cared about was safe and healthy. There was frequent texting among all of us. I began to lose momentum with writing this book. I quickly fell behind schedule as I started losing more and more focus with each passing quarantined day.

I don't know what kind of crises writers have faced when trying to finish their books. I'm sure there are many kinds, including health-related, career-related, and money-related. But I have yet to read the writer's journey memoir which discusses how they got through a national pandemic when it hit in the midst of their time working on a manuscript for a book. There certainly wasn't time for me to find such a book. To say I was flummoxed would be an understatement. Because now the demon voices of my mind were wide awake. Now there were mischievous mind gremlins wandering through my thoughts, prowling for trouble. I'd learned to reduce the volume of unproductive noise chatter over time since quitting the day job, gotten the noise of the voices down to a low rumble of background noise which I heard only vaguely while writing.

I've never lived through a national quarantine. Fear is every-fucking-where. People wearing masks and gloves. Store shelves devoid of toilet paper and paper towels. What the hell? How do I go out into the world for supplies and come home to sit down and write with what felt like pandemonium unfolding around me? *Of course*, I went down rabbit holes of googling the news in those initial days. Of course, I did. This didn't help my focus at all!

The voices rose, tall as long shadows in a dimly lit house at night: it's a fucking memoir!

Stop writing!

A memoir. From a fucking BLOG.

Just stop.

What's wrong with you? Are you blind? People are dying. And you're here playing this game? Turning your little blog into a book of essays?

Just stop.

And I was like, oh shit. Are the voices right this time? Am I wrong for trying to write this kind of book during a time like this, when the nation is facing a national crisis?

During 9/11, I had the office job and after being shut down for less than two weeks, we were all expected back to work. Once we returned, in those initial days, we didn't necessarily have to produce actual work if we didn't feel up to it. During a crisis each person tends to behave differently, finding their own ways to cope and move through it. We were colleagues, working in a big city; we didn't dare question each other's choices, even if we privately wondered about one another.

Some of us were so relieved for the distraction of our jobs that we got immediately back to working. Some of us might have preferred to stay home longer but returned to the office because we had no choice. Life was moving on, bills needed to be paid, we needed our paychecks. Some of us cried intermittently at our desk, or over the sink in the bathroom, or in a bathroom stall. We were living through a tragedy where our nation had been attacked, and our neighbors and friends had been murdered. There are no rules on how one responds during trauma's aftermath. We all do the best that we can.

At the beginning of the quarantine, I think most of us were all simply stunned to find ourselves living through something as largely unprecedented in our lifetime as a pandemic. The idea of a pandemic was for movies and sci-fi television stories, not real life. I was never a fan of such storylines. I enjoyed movies as well as the next person, but I was never enthralled with the idea of watching dramatic depictions about the end of the world as we all know it.

As the news about the mandatory government quarantine trickled down, eventually reaching us, my husband and I were more than a little dumbfounded. Almost overnight it seemed, large numbers of businesses ground to a halt, shutting their doors indefinitely to customers. Public gatherings were suddenly forbidden, suspended until further notice, all professional sporting events, canceled concerts, ceremonies like wedding receptions, and funerals. Schools were ordered closed for the rest of the school year. Gyms, spas, shopping centers, nail salons, and retail stores: all closed by order of the government. Gas stations and grocery stores, however, were to remain open. Hospitals, of course, were central to recovering from the dire health threat of the COVID-19 virus. All medical employees were considered *essential workers*. As a truck driver who moved large items of freight for a living, Howard was considered an essential worker.

On the rare occasions in the early weeks of the quarantine when I ventured out for "supplies" as groceries were now called, the streets looked eerily like a ghost town. It felt like everyone had disappeared.

What the hell? How had our lives come to this? Where were the pamphlets on guidance for adjusting to a national quarantine, like the pamphlets one might read in a medical waiting room about ailments or substance abuse? The online social media reactions felt like more pandemonium, hysteria interlacing itself through legitimate news updates and CDC warnings. There were even speculative reports about why toilet paper and paper towels were disappearing so quickly off store shelves and why Amazon's online sales were spiking in the wake of shuttering brick and mortar stores. I quickly learned to avoid the internet: it was information overload!

The voices—conflicting though they were because now the negative chatter was mixed in with the instinctual guidance upon which I often relied. I struggled to hear my gut instincts over the random self-hating chatter which had haunted my thinking since childhood—in my head were in frenzied celebration because they felt it their duty to guide me through this.

Frivolous! They hissed. Writing a memoir is frivolous.

Was it? I faltered and began to waffle. Should I be writing a book during a pandemic? Are there schools of thought on this? Are there rules I might be breaking? Is it inconsiderate to continue? After all, this job I was in—the job of book writing—was one I'd created for myself. This job was a dream chase. Where does that fall during a time like this? How might the act of writing be classified when one considers the categories of *essential* versus *non-essential* work?

Exactly! screamed my demon voices. But they didn't stop there with discouragement. I also heard things in my head like, *unwanted* and *fraud* and *unworthy*.

I started thinking maybe this time, the voices were right.

The overwhelm of our world's new normal was like a bucket of cold water thrown over me, taking me backwards, reminding me that no matter how fast I try to run, no matter how much distance I try to create between the present and the past, I would always be the damaged and broken girl-turned-woman.

But wait. I heard something else.

Another voice from within whispered, so small and so quiet, I almost missed it: *keep going.*

I know we often forget this, but death is a part of life. We're human beings. We don't get to live forever. I had to remind myself of these things. When death inevitably comes, we hurt, we grieve, but also, like it or not, we learn to accept it and move on. We who live on and learn, we must keep going.

It was a slow dawning for me when I was living through 9/11's aftermath. I remember being scared for weeks as a commuter because I had to go underground to ride the train to get from Brooklyn to Manhattan. What if we're attacked again, I wondered, trying not to panic. In those first few weeks of commuting back to work, nearly every time I rode the train and it stalled underground between stations (as is the case regularly with New York City trains), tears would spring to my eyes and I would think, maybe this is how it ends—a terrorist bomb will now blow up our train. I had to stop thinking like that. I had to move forward and begin living life again, even if the potential threat still existed. I had to keep living.

As I wrote during the quarantine, I heard the little voice in my head when she told me to keep going. But I was scared. I wasn't sure if she was right. I wasn't sure my writing was worthy enough to continue forward with this book. I was so conflicted and so confused. Because maybe (as a woman and as a mother) all I was supposed to do during this time was to simply be there for every and anyone—especially the essential workers among my loved ones—who needed an ear for listening or a shoulder to cry on.

When we got down to bare-bones basics—when I think of how I'm classified on my tax forms in terms of income status—I was just a housewife, after all. Technically, my work truly *is* non-essential, as the classification in this new reality stated. No one was paying me to write. Writing wasn't helping or providing relief efforts during our quarantine.

Suddenly, I was a small speck of a human, a microscopic dot in the huge universe, overwhelmed by it all. I burst into tears. I sobbed miserably for what felt like hours. What about me? What about my work? What about my writing dreams? Am I really supposed to quit? Do I really give this up? What about quitting my job four years ago? What would it have been for? What about all the time I put in writing?

The truth was, I didn't want to stop. I knew I needed to keep going. But how could I go on with (non-essential) writing work when everything in the world right then seemed so fucked up?

I couldn't stop.

Clearly, I didn't because this book is proof.

What I did was, I cried it out (again). And then, through a fog of sadness and despair, I reached out to an online therapist. I recognized that I needed help to get me through this quarantine as a writer who wasn't sure anymore if she deserved the writing life that she'd chosen. My therapist, Mary, reminded me of my worthiness as a woman who deserved to pursue dreams and she also rooted for my success tirelessly.

Say what?

Yes, tirelessly.

This was new for me. I'd never experienced tireless rooting for me before. It felt like a sweet maternal, balm specifically because the tireless rooting came from a woman—a *Black* woman. If I showed up in Mary's email box, weepy between appointments, she made room for me in her schedule that very day. Additionally, I could reach out to her anytime and expect a timely and interested response, the kind of response that showed how carefully she listened to what she'd learned about me from earlier sessions. I've had my share of therapy in previous seasons. This open-hearted approach was new to me and I welcomed it like the elixir that it was for my weary soul. For the first time in my life, it felt like I had a *mom*. Not a mother, a *mom*. I've never been the recipient of *mom* care before. My therapist made me feel it was acceptable to prioritize my own needs as a budding author. In addition to the small voice I heard from within, my therapist gave me the nod to keep going with writing.

In the midst of a national quarantine, I took the boldest steps I'd ever taken to preserve and protect my writing process. I sequestered myself from everyone (except Howard, of course, since we sleep in the same bed). After notifying loved ones of my determination to focus more seriously on book writing, I stopped all text exchanges. I stopped taking phone calls. I avoided visits from anyone as much as possible. I stayed off the internet. I deleted all social media apps—those addictive games! —from my phone. I significantly scaled back on trips to the grocery store, only going out twice a month when we ran low on grocery items.

I imagine to my loved ones, I looked a bit like a crazy person with my sudden reclusive lifestyle, but I was good with that. It was the only way I was going to be able to get my work done. I'm a writer. Writers are also artists. And as artists, we have the distinct tendency to do life differently than other humans on the planet.

10

FEAR AS MY RIDE-OR-DIE CHICK

As a young teenager, I was terrified of my father.

It's safe to say, my father was the first person to properly introduce me to *fear*, to bring my awareness sharply into focus on the concept of fear. It shouldn't have been him because as a parent, his job was to protect and make me feel safe. It should have been spiders. It should have been the monster I imagined was in my closet or under my bed after lights out. It should have been strangers, the thought of being kidnapped. But nope. Fear first nestled itself deeply in my heart thanks to him.

I think I understand what my parents were trying to teach us when it came to fear, particularly as Black people in America. I'm torn. I know, how can I be torn? Either you terrorized your kids or you didn't. Um, yes and no. Sometimes Blackness is complicated.

I'm torn because now I have a dual perspective as a daughter and a mother. My children are now adults. I made a lot of mistakes, but I'm satisfied with the job I did in light of my sorely lacking preparation. I'm not saying my parents were right. They weren't. I'm saying, I understand what they were trying to do.

I think my parents got *fear* and *respect* mixed up, possibly saw it as synonymous at times. I'm not proud of this part of the parenting job I myself did, but in my defense, it was, in fact, a learned behavior. And it was probably the same for my parents although, they definitely took it too far. Hell, a lot of us did as Black authority figures in our homes. Sometimes the powerless gets a taste of power and lose their logical sense of balance. My parents were obsessed with being shown respect by their children. They wanted us to demonstrate proper respect for authority and hierarchy so that when we moved into our individual futures as adults, we'd be good rule-followers. And in their mind, rule-followers (eventually) got rewarded. (This turns out to be mortally untrue for Black people, especially in 2020.)

Showing fear and respect in the face of authority—in the skewed viewpoints of members of a violent household—was the right thing to do because it garnered brownie points and (supposedly, also) more respect. I tweaked this lesson to the tune of less violence in my own home. It didn't turn out well. My children would grow into adults who would go on to rightly delineate for me how I'd failed them with my learned fear/respect approaches. As hard as I'd tried to avoid being like my parents, I still managed to take on some of their ways, carrying bad habits into my own parenting life. I'm not proud of this. I was, at times, a bit of a bully. I'm so sorry that I was this way.

I'm looking back with a desire to understand how I lost my way, how I occasionally slid so easily into the bully lane of life.

When he wasn't drinking and was in a good mood, my father was the type who smiled easily. If life had gone differently for him—maybe if he wasn't born Black or if he wasn't born to a teenage parent or if he wasn't left by his mother at age eight to be raised and beaten often by a grandmother who hated him for reasons unknown—he showed the potential to be incredibly successful and irresistibly charming. But even when he was in a good mood, I knew enough as a kid to tread carefully when dealing with him because the slightest provocation could be interpreted as an imagined assault on his authority, even if the provocation came from a blaring car horn on the street outside our home. I just never knew. And sometimes he also surprised me—surprised all of us in the family—with benevolence, with a kind of calm normalcy we were unaccustomed to in the shadow of an often-violent home.

When you realize your life is a prison—such as I had become painfully aware of by age thirteen—you become willing to take risks in order to eke out good moments when and wherever you can find it. Good moments cultivated by a prisoner becomes a way to feel human, a way to feel normal.

I strove to cultivate good moments as a way to feel a part of ordinary kid life. Being in school was my favorite place to be. More often than not, it's usually abused kids—those of us who were abused via violence and/or neglect; those of us, also for example, who ate our most healthy and hearty meals during school hours— who tend to love school to the point of wanting to be there all the time. The other kids, those with at least a moderately safe and content home life, are easily bored with too much time spent in school. Boredom is a luxury of the well-cared-for offspring. And so, I enjoyed school in an irrational way.

There was nothing my parents could do about that kind of happiness in my youthful existence. Despite their unabashed reign of violence over us, my parents were also law-abiding citizens hung up on appearances. They lived a life of flagrant pretense.

It makes sense that I would explore a child's (not unusual) vocation of telling lies. Lying was also a way of life in my household. Where there is dysfunction, there tends to be delusion. And when we are deluding our own selves, unable to admit the truth of our circumstances, rationalizing irrational behavior, we're forming the habit of telling lies.

There came a day when I concocted the biggest lie of my teenaged life and after rehearsing the lie over and over again, I told it to my father in prayerful hope that I'd be believed. Of course, up to that point, I'd had plenty of practice in the lying department. I was a teenager, after all. It's what teenagers do. Especially teenagers who feel like prisoners in their own home. Especially a teenager who felt helpless in the face of abusive authority. We do whatever little outlaw shit we can think of as a way to take back our agency (apparently, this continues well into adulthood, especially for the disenfranchised and marginalized).

But this lie that I told as an eighth-grader had way too many layers and way too many moving parts to hold up in the court of my psychotically unpredictable father. And also, what I didn't know at the time was, I was too unpracticed with lying to him. I was waaayyy out of my league because I was lying to a grown-ass man who was himself, quite well-versed in the art of lying, an OG veteran of victimized circumstance.

What happened was, I wanted to visit my friend Noah in the hospital after school. My memory is hazy on this, but I think Noah was in some kind of car accident. I can remember his arm being in a cast as he lay in the hospital bed smiling at me. I can remember the contrast of his dark brown skin against the light green dotted white hospital gown they'd put him in.

But mostly, I remember his smile because Noah had large white teeth that were perfectly straight. He was a few years older than me and there was stubble on his face to indicate this. I adored Noah because he treated me with respect, unlike most teenage boys I had met up to that point in my young life. We didn't have a term in our youthful lexicon for *rape culture,* but that way of life felt palpable around me during my middle and high school days. As girls, many of us often felt the male gaze upon our bodies long before we even fully understood our own sexuality. I was underdeveloped physically, but the girls I went to school with were often mistaken for being older than they were. However, it didn't matter if you were curvaceous like some of my peers or if you were a flat-chested string-bean like me. Girls received male attention simply for being female. It seemed like none of us could walk down a block without some boy or grown-ass man cat-calling or leering in our direction.

We were residents of a large, bustling city populated with competing personalities. Sure, there were quiet and respectful boys, boys who never cat-called, boys who cared more about their schoolwork and playing with their friends, boys who showed both genders the respect taught to them by loving parents. But who noticed those boys? Those boys were as noticeable as the backup singers on a hit song.

I didn't notice Noah, he noticed me. Under his gaze, I felt like someone whose ideas might actually matter. I knew zip about being flirty. I avoided my own sexuality like it was something harmful. Noah was someone I looked up to in the same way you would look up to a big brother. I don't know if Noah had sisters he was in the habit of protecting or if he was super close to his mother or what, but he wasn't like so many of the guys in his age group. This was the 1980s and most teenage men were posturing for respect, competing with each other constantly for female attention. Unfortunately, many of them thought the best way to go about this was to lead with their libidos.

Noah was not this way. When I talked, he actually listened, and he didn't look away from my face like someone trying to hide motives. He made me feel safe. So when I heard from mutual friends that he was in an accident that landed him in the hospital, I was determined to visit, to let him know I was concerned about his recovery. I didn't know how bad he was hurt, but I wanted to see for myself. I also wanted to reciprocate the kindness I'd been shown by him.

Here was an instance where pretending to be an ordinary kid from a normal family became problematic. It's not like I had normal parents whose permission I could seek with reasonable expectation of approval to visit my friend in the hospital. There were too many strikes against me in this situation: first and foremost, the fact that Noah was a male. The second, I was in middle school and Noah was in high school. Our school buildings were directly across the street from each other. And finally, not that this makes a difference when dealing with irrational lunatics in the parenting role, my parents didn't *know* Noah. In fact, they'd never even heard of him. Never seen him on our street. He may as well have been a pen-pal from Australia or Riker's Island; it would have been all the same to them.

Back then, my father had recently become an entrepreneur, which meant he was often at home. Unless I cut school—I hadn't developed the courage to do this yet, but it would be a surety in another year or two— there was no way to visit Noah in the hospital without getting home late. And by late, I mean 5:00 instead of 3:30. What'd I tell you? Prisoner.

There was just no other way around it, I *had* to lie. And I needed to make it a good lie. The thing about lying that all good liars know is, keep it simple. Clearly, this wisdom had not reached my weirdly sheltered— because although I was an abused kid, I knew very little about the outside world, other than what lying American television was teaching me—existence. Therefore, I concocted a fucking whopper of a story. The story basically went like this: there I was, waiting at the bus stop to take the usual route home via city bus when a terrible car accident happened right in front of me. I was a witness to the horrific scene. When the police arrived, I was detained to provide my eye-witness version of the events.

I know. Pathetic.

Later on that day, somewhere close to 5:30, as I stood before my blankly staring father, I began sweating profusely and trembling like a deer with a rifle scope's dot on her body. But I managed to push the ridiculous concocted story through my lips. There were long stretches of silence whenever I stopped talking at intervals during the telling. My father's expression was deadpan. He barely blinked as he stared into my face from his leisurely perch in a straight back chair in the den. Finally, his mouth twitched into something resembling a repressed smile. My galloping heart would not be tamed by this unusual break in facial muscles.

My father pointed out that I was trembling and then he told me to go to my room.

And that was it.

No yelling. No beating. No warnings about the next time.

I'd told a clumsy, oversized lie and gotten away with it because it was so inane and so unbelievable, rather than invite my father's wrath, it amused him. I think it amused him more to see me squirm like a worm on a hook. The story itself, probably not so much.

I'm guessing my father decided he didn't really care what the real story was. On that day, he saw a teenager telling him a rambling story filled with lies. How much energy might it cost him to get to the truth at the bottom of it? As a parent now myself, I belong to a club of humans on the planet who'd be so grateful their kid was safely home, the real story wouldn't have mattered. Could my father have thought this too? Who knows? Whatever his motives were, he showed his more benevolent side in that moment. There may have been a little bit of ordinary parent in him after all. He wasn't all irrational violence and predatory leanings.

As crazy as it may sound, my father's response helped me sustain my own pretense of "normal kid" for Noah. As a young teenager, I'd taken a risk for the sake of looking normal and it paid off.

Noah recovered from his injuries and went on to graduate from high school a year later. I never saw or spoke with him again. He would never know what I risked to visit him, how much courage it took, and how much fear was induced because of my actions. If I was the fainting kind, I would have collapsed on the floor in mid-explanation to my father that day, I was *that* afraid.

This kind of fear still visits me today. This kind of fear has visited me over and over on the dream-chasing and writing journey.

And I hate it. I hate the way *fear* makes me feel, how it can still make my heart race, make my pores sweat, and bring small tremors to my body. It gives me a feeling of helplessness. I don't spend a lot of time dwelling in the past, reflecting on the unpleasant experiences of childhood. But when I'm frightened, I do experience feelings that I recognize, feelings that remind me of bygone powerlessness.

Fear is merely one emotion among many in our human makeup. And yet, no other emotion is exploited in American society with as much pervasiveness as *fear*. On the road to writing this book, I've gone out of my way to read as many memoirs as I could find and feel resonance with. That second part—resonance—has been no easy task. All memoirs are *not* alike.

I appreciate that a wider variety of memoirs are available these days. I know I'm in the minority when it comes to my appreciation for memoirs. Most people—no matter how much they love to read books—hate reading memoirs. In the last two decades, memoirs have basically inundated the literary world even though most people avoid reading them in the same way most of us tend to avoid liquid cold medicine (capsule, please!). But I like them. As an older book reader, I've turned a corner on the kinds of books I typically enjoy, preferring nonfiction over fiction nowadays. In my younger days, except for an occasional celebrity biography, I was loathed to read nonfiction. Ugh! True stories? No way. I thought they were too boring. But memoirs have changed in the 2000s. Writers have loosened up, mixing their own vulnerability with good storytelling. Thank goodness!

Recently, as I was reading a memoir by a white female journalist, I was intrigued by something she wrote that explained some of her own fears about writing a memoir. The writer—a millennial—has well over a decade of journalism experience via online news blogs, online magazines, and print publications. And yet, despite all that experience, she is well aware of how "real writers" are inclined to sneer at personal essays.

I had to resist the message of fear she was carrying in that section of her memoir. Of course, I realize she didn't write that to be discouraging to other writers—like me! —of personal essays. The writer was simply being honest about how it felt to be writing something as personal and as vulnerable as a memoir. And it was a reminder to me about how deliberate The World is—the world that we *all* live in, not just writers—about inducing fear to keep us stymied in our comfortable ruts of survival living.

Fear is my constant companion. I have to work really hard to battle through my fears to get work done. And the thing is, this is something that all human beings already have to deal with. But we on the margins get extra doses of it heaped on us seemingly every other day at so many constant turns of situations in our collective and individual lives. And the really shitty result is, some of us are full of fear all the time! As Black women, we fear the tenuous safety of our Black men, how easily the color of their skin might draw the ire of the next ignorant racist. We get reminders on an all too frequent basis on how grounded in fact, how reasonable that fear actually is. George Floyd, to name one recent example.

My reality as a Black woman pursuing writing dreams is a jarring attempt at audaciousness. Like, who the hell do you think you are, Mia? How dare you step out of your lane? You with your lack of credentials (even though I have them), you with your lack of experience (I have some of that too), and your personal history littered with damage and brokenness. How dare you?

That's not to say that there aren't brilliant examples of Black men and women who have defied their own difficult or challenging circumstances to overcome the odds against them in an environment that has been historically hostile against them to produce great achievements. But statistically speaking, the odds are still NOT in our favor as people of color. Statistically speaking, the numbers of successful Blacks across all American commerce and art industries are still small enough to make dream-chasing from the margins seem almost delusional.

It's an awful feeling to be full of fear so often. Frankly, it pisses me off. I can still remember wanting my father to die when I was a kid. I'm not proud of this either, but I used to pray that he would be killed in a car accident for a couple of years during my youth. At the time, I thought it was a reasonable ask because he was someone who frequently got drunk and drove home from bars. I thought he was a hazard to our family and to the community. It seemed like an okay prayer back then. But really, it was just one child's helpless cry for help.

Now here I am, all grown up, feeling very thankful that those prayers were never answered. In addition, now here I am, all grown up, belatedly pursuing dreams and realizing how truly difficult it is. The difficulty I feel is not only because I'm an older person, but also because I'm a Black woman, and the odds against my success feels increasingly restrictive.

It's baffling to have to keep wrapping one's mind around the flagrancy of frequent white apathy in the face of American racism—meaning, laws which do not protect us from the imbalance of accessible resources and also, laws which do not protect us against violence to our bodies. Not that I think white people don't care. I know some of them care because I've had relationships with enough white people to know that I've been loved, thought of, and cared about by some of the angels among them. However, individual love from one person to another hasn't been enough to translate to a society's parity. Black people are still not safe. And yet, I am still hopeful because this place, America, is my home.

I don't have the luxury of giving up. Because that's what giving up would feel like to me: a luxury. As if no one else on the planet might be harboring the dream of a better life. As if my story, this writer's journey and all the turns it has taken, might not be the hope another dream-chasing person could cling to. Fuck being practical, holding on to your day job. Fuck racism.

This book is also about possibilities. It's about the idea of someone—telling the truth as she saw and experienced it—writing her way through one of the hardest times of not only her own life, but also the lives of other Americans. I'm not my race. I'm not my childhood experiences. I'm more than those fragments of life seasons, no matter how long and wide they may have stretched. I'm so much more.

I'm an entirely whole person. And I refuse to be cowed by *fear*, the *fear* of my occasionally triggered heart and the *fear* of the world. Under more important conditions, *fear* is my ride or die chick. But I've learned: I am the boss. Contrary to popular machinations employed by our social system, *fear* does not get to control my life.

Fear may ride with me, but she has to ride as a passenger while *I* do the driving. Not the other way around.

11

I LEAPT—I'M ALREADY GONE
[*Excerpt #3: OBM Blog – February 2018*]

I wish I could have taken you with me. But mine was a solo journey. It had to be that way.

When I packed up all my things to leave, to take this leap of faith, I didn't realize I'd be going without you. I wish you could see things the way I do, that I could lend you my heart, my mind, and my eyes, even if only for a few minutes.

When we *don't* talk, I can feel myself slipping away from you. And when we *do* talk, I can see how far apart we've drifted. Isn't that strange?

One day, about four years ago, after several weeks of failed attempts at connecting with so many of the women around me — because women are the biggest deal, in my estimation — Hubby and I were supposed to be getting dressed to go out. My outfit was hanging in the closet, shoes were waiting on the floor nearby. All I had left to do was get dressed. But on that morning, a lump had been forming in my throat, and my eyes stung. After much procrastination, I turned to Hubby and whispered, can we just *not* go?

On that day, we stayed home and he let me bawl in his arms like a tired toddler.

Even as I tried to explain through the sobs, tried to talk through the hiccups, and the miserable retching, and even as Hubby nodded sympathetically, I doubt he really understood what in the world had brought all that on. And yet, he was good enough to simply hold me and act as if every word I choked out made logical sense. Always my angel, that man.

From that day forward, I developed a tendency towards quietness in the company of others.

Bit by bit, in small steps—reluctantly at first—I began the journey towards my truer self. It never occurred to me that in taking such a journey, I'd be leaving many of my love-people behind. I just knew I was dying inside; it felt as if I couldn't breathe.

For years, we'd all been talking and smiling, eating and laughing, watching and promising, until none of it made much sense to me anymore. I merely smiled so I wouldn't look crazy, to hide that I wanted to scream, and then I'd lean in for a hug with someone until I could blink back the inconvenient tears.

Those days are done. Now I am living a more authentic life.

I'm gone. Yet I keep looking back to find that you're not with me. It occurs to me you probably won't be along anytime soon. That's a tough one, a hard pill I didn't know I would have to swallow.

Life, right? Our journeys can take different turns, at different times, and in different seasons. How can I make you see as I do now or feel what I am feeling anew? I can't. It's like this: As the night approaches, one of us laments the day's end, while the other is excited for a dark sky peppered with stars. And as a new day dawns, one of us is thinking about *time* while another languishes in a *moment*. I am gone. And I have no plans to return. I didn't think this through when I was packing up everything in my heart to take that leap.

That leap of faith. The journey. I leapt without looking. And now, I am gone.

I can think of no encouraging words to offer. I can make no promises about our tomorrows. All I can say is, I wish you peace and happiness—it's what I've finally found. When I think about those situations I once felt so tied to, it makes me sad. I'm thankful for the place I'm in today. Connected to universal energy, the divine flow moving through us all, never to feel disconnected from anyone or anything ever again, never to feel lost, dislodged, or confused. I have only to close my eyes to remember all that I already have and all that I will never again be without.

And yet, I'm still startled to find us standing apart. Another explanation missing from the invisible book of life— what to do when we take journeys that lead us away from loved ones, our blood-ties, and our friends. How to move along the uncommon ground upon which we stand. How to agree to disagree and continue to love one another deeply while swirling along the underbelly of newly divergent outlooks. Awkward silences, stolen glances, lingering looks.

However, intuition tells me it's not the end of the world for any of us. Like the rush of a strong river, we flow, digress, break off into separate streams, and then converge for the gentle, meandering slosh into larger bodies. A lake or an ocean. If the Earth is okay with this, then who are we to question such natural order? We go on. We love harder. We reach higher. And if we can believe, we all get our chance to win.

I used to panic and flail in some relationships, gripping until one of us faced the threat of drowning. I'm not that woman anymore. I used to say, "Wait! Don't grow so fast. I'm not ready, I must catch up." Or I'd make a silent promise to stay put, slow my own growing to a crawl, or even shrink to make myself fit into someone else's mold. Sisters forever, loyal daughter, dutiful mother, best friends for life, a new community home for good—failing to understand that *change must come*, no matter what. We evolve, constantly moving forward.

One day something beautiful happened. I stopped living in shame and being consumed by fear. I took a deep breath and emerged, face tilted to the sun, blessed, smiling, and bathed in loving light.

Let's let go of each other so we can fly. Let's stop dragging each other down. It's not enough if only one of us to let go. If I let go, you have to let go too. Be who you are. Be the amazing person you were born to be. The world is spinning without a pause button, so we may as well enjoy the ride.

I'm already gone. And life feels really good.

12

LET'S TALK ABOUT LOVE!
[*Excerpt #4: OBM Blog—March 2019*]

You may find this hard to believe, but … I know some things about you. As people, you and I are not that much different.

You're searching for something more and you're not opposed to taking your search to unusual places for reading material. It could be in magazines or in pamphlets or in the pages of books unheard of to most of us. In the pouch on the backseat of planes and trains. In a waiting room or in the bathroom of a home not yours. You're almost always on the lookout for the hidden answers of an often-confusing world.

You seek something more because you know you deserve it in your heart, you deserve better than what you already have. Also, there's a lot more to you than what others see and think they know about you. In other words, you're kind of a big deal, someone pretty special. So you go to lesser-known places for affirmation. This is why seekers seek and why artists create. We are in perpetual exchange with our longings and our findings.

I used to be the most insecure person I knew. I used to put on a front to convince people that I belonged, that I knew what I was doing, and convince them that I was trustworthy and reliable.

Beneath my front of pseudo-confidence, the truth is, I saw myself as damaged goods unworthy of anyone's time. I had parents who likely felt that way about themselves and as a result, couldn't show me healthy love. Their inability to show me love thoroughly fucked up my head until I eventually fell to pieces and began the real work of putting myself back together in middle-age.

Thankfully, beneath the front I presented there lived and breathed a little girl who knew who she was born to be. All babies begin their lives feeling worthy and expectant. It's in our primal nature to know who we are at the beginning. We don't need our greatness or our beauty to be explained to us. However, with the onslaught of our environment, depending on what we learn, we often forget how lovely we were at birth.

The little person inside me never left. For more than five decades my inner-child has been whispering. Along the way sometimes I heard her but, more often—too many times to count—I did not.

While on the writing journey, an idea came to me through meditation. I was inspired to go on a *love-journey* in order to become more deliberate about my expressions of love. Once I began this *love-journey*, it was like someone handed my innerchild a megaphone. I began hearing her loud and clear with unprecedented consistency.

I think we're *all* on love-journeys whether we realize it or not. We were made with Love—regardless of the circumstances of conception—by virtue of what a woman's body goes through to develop each person. The birth mother could be depressed or elated, murderous or nurturing, her body will still do all the life-giving things a body does to grow life. That process is a miracle and that miracle is Love. In our humanness, we yearn for love's replenishment the way a body craves food and water. We respond with an instinctual pull in the face of Love—or any act of kindness—shown to us.

There came a time when I had to stop following so closely all the trending activities of The World because it just wasn't working for me anymore. I had to take a long look at myself and figure out why I was experiencing inexplicable moods which often swung in high and low extremes, from sadness to irritation to rage to indifference to joy and back down again.

Now that I'm older and wiser, I understand that all of the answers we seek about life can be found within each of us. So I meditate. And I've gotten into the habit of listening to my heart—trusting more in my instincts—whenever she speaks.

However, I must admit there've been times when I didn't always like what my heart was telling me to do. You know what I mean? It's like when you know you were wrong in a situation and you hate to admit it. And then your realize you owe someone an apology. Ugh. Yeah, like that.

Along came the inspiration for getting on a *love-journey* and I hesitated.

I hesitated because I thought if I had to be all about love every day, then I couldn't be my weirdly annoying but lovable, occasionally shitty behaving self. I thought I had to clean up my act completely. And initially, I resisted. I honestly thought my inner-voice was wrong or that maybe I was putting words into my own mind, manipulating the meditation. I thought a *love-journey* would require too much good behavior on my part and I was like, fuck that.

Turns out, I didn't have to choose either/or. A quest towards acting more loving is not a quest towards perfection. Being more loving doesn't mean I give up my asshole side. I like being kind, thoughtful, and all the other good things. But I also like the jerk in me because she has her good points too, including a willingness to go into battle for me without hesitation whenever I need her.

When I first started writing on my blog back in March 2018, I was struggling with emotions, often triggered by the friendship research. My favorite part of the research had been sitting down and listening to all the different stories the women were sharing. But when it was time to research the *clinical* and *academic* side of things, I became uncomfortable and apprehensive because this stirred my insecurities. I didn't think I was smart enough or had enough credentials to query academic individuals.

I was definitely up to the task. I just didn't have enough self-belief yet.

Who said anything about self-esteem and confidence? All I ever wanted to do was write. Why did self-esteem and confidence have to play such a crucial part in the writing formula? What was with all the emotions bubbling up and making my insides swirl? As I tried to focus, pressing myself to get on with the work and write regardless of feeling triggered, the tears came again.

My inner-guides had shown up in meditation to help, to offer guidance, pointing me in the direction of the dreaded *love-journey*. I didn't even know what a *love-journey* looked like. Was it like a tour? Was it what musicians and comedians did, performing in various cities, at different stops? I didn't have the funds to travel around, so I figured that couldn't be what I was expected to do.

I couldn't ignore the inner-guides because love-journey thoughts refused to leave my mind. Those thoughts kept popping up no matter what I was doing, from routine chores to recreation to work. I *had* to do it, whether I understood what it was or not.

So I fudged like I usually do when I don't know the answers, figuring it out as I went along. I did the things I thought were required of someone on a *love-journey*. I smiled more often at strangers. And if—while on line at the grocery check-out or sitting in the waiting room for a doctor's visit—a random stranger made small talk to fill the silence (something that used to irritate the crap out of me), I chatted back with actual enthusiasm. I was determined to give the *love-journey* my best effort.

I complimented random female strangers on things I saw about them which I liked—earrings, hairstyles, blouses, sneakers, boots, dresses, cell phone cases, even their smiles. In one scenario, that last bit once brought me a side-eye like, no lady, you are *not* my type.

A lot of the responses to my kindness were pleasant; some even responded with delighted surprise. But there were a few strangers who either flat out ignored me or thanked me warily, glancing around for security should the need arise. Some days it felt good and some days, I felt like a complete loser.

I journaled my way through the experience. I wrote about the people I met, the strangers who smiled, the strangers who scowled, and the conversations I got into. I wrote about how it was all making me feel. It wasn't all as bad as I thought. Eventually, something inside of me began to shift. This shift happened in such a subtle way at first, I almost missed it.

In the beginning, I assumed a *love-journey* meant more patience and charitable behavior on my part towards other people. I thought the journey had to do with being more like Jesus or Buddha or something. That was part of it, but not all of it. Yes, the point was to be more loving, but not just to others around me. I was also meant to be more loving to my SELF.

I tried this: acted kinder to myself, turned down the volume on self-bashing thoughts, times when I scolded myself for not knowing something or choosing badly. And I cranked my love-dial way up, turning a glow of love onto myself, shining the light of it in my own face every single day. I greeted myself in the mirror each day, looked into my own eyes, and said, *I love you, Mia.* I smiled at myself, saying, *good job* when I did something right, and *that's okay, my love* whenever I made mistakes.

I began to change. Wow! Something inside my being began to stir. I started feeling loved in a deeper way. It was like I met someone special, like I was dating a new person or got adopted into an extra family.

Positive mantras and slogans, the popular recent trends employed as tools for self-love, are barely effective beginnings for really getting into the act of loving yourself. What I now understand as a logical truth is that self-loving actions must be as deliberate and meticulous as the love shown to a new infant or a new lover.

Our social system has done a number on our collective and individual minds when it comes to our understanding of the concept of Love. There've been so many mixed messages. I can see why the announcement of a love-journey might be met with skepticism.

Love is the basis of all human accomplishments because love is at the root of every single creation. It begins with the passion which inspires an idea and becomes the sequential actions which the idea creates. Examples range from a crocheted mitten to the design of a skyscraper, from the lines of a poem to the construction of a bridge, from the writing of a web design to the cultivation of medical cures, and on it has gone throughout the ages.

Social dictates around Love have wreaked a bit of havoc and confusion, causing us to hesitate and question ourselves when our hearts have always known what to do. We've actually been led to believe that there can be such a thing as too much love. Men especially are watched closely for too much love in their behavior lest they be perceived as having too much feminine energy inside them (ha! they should be so lucky).

All of us, women *and* men, have been schooled that love is to be tamped down or offered sparingly beyond our intimate circles. If there is too much of it, you might be viewed as a bible-thumper or Jesus-freak or gullible, naive prey, deserving of any predatory machinations which befall you.

Also, in recent years—based on what I've seen of the past decade, especially in online campaigns against this—there's been an enormous movement *against* self-love. The word *narcissism* has been wielded like a weapon on blogs, on social media, in movies, on television, and in books. Society has made it one of their top priorities to police our self-love activities. Too many selfies? Despicable. Self-congratulating? Heinous. Self-prioritizing? Selfish. Self-promoting? Too much ego. Self-assured? Hubris.

I started to see myself differently: I'm not so dumb, after all. I'm not the fool The World had succeeded in making me think I was. I realized that my ideas could actually be valid. My brain works as well as any scientist or doctor or lawyer. It's simply a matter of using it or losing it just like any other body part we're born with.

We're simply human beings in a human family. We each need Love. Even if we don't frolic in acts of Love every day, even if there's only the memory of its sensation which sustains us, none of us can thrive without having experienced some semblance of Love.

I didn't merely imagine an anti-self-love campaign among us; it's not a fantasy that I made up. It exists! It isn't an accident that so many of us are awkward around excess kindness and loving acts in the company of strangers or casual acquaintances (unless there's a tragedy. It's acceptable for us to be loving with strangers during near-death accidents and mass destruction). There are implicit social rules around Love and most of us follow them, whether we realize it or not.

My four biggest Love-journey lessons are:

1. Love can't be mastered or exhausted, hence, there's no end to how deep any of us can go with our love. The reset button on being loving must be hit every single day and we begin the practice of expressing love all over again.

2. The World wants us to fail. Not only does The World want us to fail, it wants us to fail spectacularly so that it can be there to pick us up when we fall. As a remedy for our wounds, The World offers consumerism as a quick fix. Like addicts, we are ever in pursuit of that first high, buying cars and homes and designer clothes to give us that endorphin-like feeling of accomplishment. And if those things don't work or are unaffordable, there is also food, alcohol, makeup, apps, porn, and a litany of

other less costly, distracting paraphernalia to keep us occupied.

3. Our social structure is designed to keep us inept and bungling at Love. We are discouraged from practicing Love consistently across a broad spectrum of life's activities. If we adhere to social dictates about Love, we will restrict our loving attitudes to family, friends, and the close-knit circles which inevitably shrink as we age. And since for the majority of us, 75 to 90 percent of our time is usually spent at jobs, in school, at chores, and attending to life's errands, we will spend more time engaging in *loveless* activities than in *loving* ones. During the considerably smaller downtime that we each have at our disposal to be more freely loving, we become less practiced at it. Consequently, we have the tendency to unintentionally hurt the people we love the most without understanding why.

4. You have everything you need in order to be, have, and do anything you desire in this world. You were born with all that you need inside of you. No matter what kind of challenge or difficulty you face, all of the solutions lie within you. You are brilliant! The world works mightily to keep you from knowing this fact.

* * *

I didn't know when I went on the *love-journey* that it would become such a gamechanger for my life. I would become the most impressive version of myself I'd ever expressed as. The *love-journey* turned me into a badass boss. In a world that hates women more than it loves them—patriarchy! —this has been a miraculous turn of perspective for a formerly broken woman like me. Being a badass boss doesn't mean I stop facing bouts of insecurity. I learned how to navigate through them, just like all the other feelings we experience as humans. My message to anyone—regardless of gender, race, class, or sexual orientation—is, if someone like me can discover and believe in her own badassery bossness, ANYONE can discover and believe in theirs too. It all begins and ends with Love.

13

WHAT KIND OF SEXY AM I?
[Excerpt #5: OBM Blog – May 2019]

Do I think I'm sexy? Have I ever oozed sex appeal? At what point did I begin to really strut my stuff?

It's funny how so many of us women will look at each other and immediately jump to conclusions. *Oh, I don't like her. Oh, she's definitely drama. Oh, she thinks she's hot shit. I do not trust her at all.* Right? As women living in the patriarchy, I'm willing to bet we've all had one or more of these thoughts by the time we hit our mid-twenties.

Because inside patriarchal culture—where every industry and system are male-centric by default and by design—women are inevitably pitted against one another, and competition propels us into fighting over scraps. We've gotten into the habit of thinking there's not enough for all of us. Not enough men, not enough jobs, not enough standards of beauty, not enough money, not enough food, not enough love, not enough ways into better living .... not enough *anything*. Additionally—for the heterosexual women among us— more than all else, we tend to feel there are definitely not enough men. So we give each other side-eyes, often distrusting each other impulsively.

And when you feel as if you're always on the outside, looking in, as I'd felt for years, you often vacillate between feeling combative and feeling apologetic. Combative because territories need defending and apologetic because you feel guilty if it appears you have more than someone else.

I was rarely an angel in earlier seasons, even when I presented as a meek or patient person. Privately, in my heart, swallowed rage made me buck like an untamed horse. For years the world's groundwork often felt as if it was peppered with landmines and nowhere felt safe for stepping. As I progressed into young adulthood, feeling little to no love at home, I discovered that the outside world was usually just as lacking in love— sometimes even hateful and hostile—as my home was. Friendly enemies, friendly friends, hostile enemies, and hostile friends. It was all pretty fucking confusing.

In addition to figuring out how we women were supposed to relate to each other, there was also the conundrum of figuring out how to interact with men. Some you wanted to date, but most you simply wanted to share a parallel existence with sans feeling ogled, accosted, or misunderstood. What did I know in my twenties? With no older woman to guide me, I relied on my peers; and we could only speculate on answers between the sexes.

What was this thing called *sexuality*? Did I have it? Initially, I thought, nope. Not even a little bit. I was too skinny, especially in Black culture. High school friends would sometimes tease me about how thin I was. I had no curves in the hip area other than the traditional fledgling Black-girl booty. Boobs? Umm, nope, not much to speak of anyway. It was hard to feel sexy while being caught between conflicting and competing definitions of sexuality.

It always felt like everyone around me understood more than I did about sexuality, while I seemed to frequently be running on late or empty with my own awareness. As a girl missing her mother's involvement or interest, I was fixated on all the other women around me. Especially if they seemed confident in their own sexuality. I thought, fascinating! I couldn't figure out what they had that I didn't. So I mimicked, trying on and taking off attitudes like makeup.

Thirty years into adulthood, I've finally learned how to be comfortable in my own skin. It's all still new, but I'm working the hell out of my gifts before they fade away with age and disuse. No more shrinking. No more making myself smaller in hopes that women will appreciate this and like me more as a result. Fuck that.

My journey has been a long one. Life hasn't been easy, and though the current seasons are now kinder and more love-filled, I'm mindful of this fact: it wasn't always thus.

As a fifty-something-year-old woman, it occurs to me, I've already lost enough time neglecting to preen and revel in my own beauty and sexuality. I've spent a ridiculous amount of time thinking that society—more specifically, other women—would one day pat me on the back for appearing humble and chaste. These days I've banished such thinking.

Not only do I rock, I rock too much to go on pretending that I don't. It would do more of us good to embrace the entirety of how we each actually rock.

I don't rock because I look like someone else's idea of beautiful. I rock because I can now behold my own reflection without feeling the shameful pull to look away when I look in the mirror. I rock because I can finally lock eyes with myself and say the words, *I love you*. I rock because I finally love the skin I am in.

What changed? I stopped taking my cues from the outside world and finally began listening to the wisdom from within. *I* changed. I burned it all down to begin again. It was the only way for me to find myself, the only way for me to figure out who I really am.

Am I Sexy? Oh, yes indeed! So sexy, I radiate. But this is a different kind of sexy. The sexy I'm radiating isn't restricted to the fuckability definition of traditional patriarchal fare. Nah! That's silly locker room, I-wish-I-had-a-bigger-dick-cuz-I'm-embarrassed-by-my-small-dick, trash talk.

The Sexy that I'm talking about is rooted in the Sexiness definition I discovered in middle-age. My Sexy is primarily loaded with sober intelligence, open-heartedness, and more often than not, my Sexy is devoid of shame. My sexy doesn't hope for acceptance or approval, my Sexy just *is*. My Sexy is beautiful on the outside because of the vast beauty which exists on the inside.

How did I figure this out? I burned down my mental house and reconstructed my thinking from the ground up. It's a process that continues. And like everyone else, as long as I'm alive, I am never done. I am a work in progress.

14

MY SEXUAL HEALING

I learned a long time ago, as a girl with a diary, the healing power of writing down the secrets of my heart, giving myself permission to speak when no invitations for my opinion were extended. When I ventured to share thoughts with The World, it began by confiding in two close friends in high school, venturing to expose my vulnerabilities by speaking secrets with the hope of finding affirmation. It worked. I discovered others who had similar experiences and some who shared my outlooks.

I took the sharing of my thoughts a little further. In the lecture halls on college campus, I dared to raise my hand and offer commentary—even though this was extremely rare for me, at least I tried—and was shocked to see a professor nod in agreement or another one admit to being introduced to a new perspective. But college classrooms are not real life. Once I was in the world of work, as I moved into careers and professional settings—populated mainly by white people—I started making adjustments to the way I spoke, the way I dressed, and the ideas I had. The more the years passed—seeing the way routines I'd learned at home and values I believed in so often clashed with the world I was inhabiting—the quieter I became.

I learned to adapt, not realizing that I would lose track of what in my behavior was inspired by my own instincts and what was driven by my desperate need to fit in with The World.

I got so lost at various turns of seasons, I even forgot how to use my voice on a blank page, forgot what I wanted to say when I journaled, forgot how to be honest about my joy and my pain as a way to figure out the complicated and confusing episodes I was experiencing. Once I got lost, the core aspect of my sexuality seemed to vanish, leaving me with only the base instincts of a sexual appetite. I never imagined that this would become a thing of interest for me to examine eventually, that it would be a resulting layer of having survived rape in the patriarchy's rape culture.

I'd been sexually abused by my biological father for most of my childhood. The rapes and sexual assaults by my father didn't end until I was sixteen, the age I finally realized that no one was going to save me if I didn't save myself. Sixteen was the age I first struck out, taking a stand against my family by calling the police and turning my father in for his assaults on my body. I had tried to wait to be saved, hoping it would be my mother—she stumbled in on a raping episode when I was thirteen—who saved me, but my waiting was in vain. When I saw the choice I would have to make—my life, my body, and what was left of my childhood—saw how terrible it was, how it came down to choosing either myself or my family, I did what I knew I had to do to take my body back.

But I didn't fully take back my body until I was well into middle age. There were so many layers of emotional and psychological recovery to attend to, I had no idea that there might be areas of recovery which might have been overlooked, areas that I neglected as I attended therapy in brief intervals throughout the years. How would I have known? Who would have stepped in and told me what to look out for as I moved from girlhood to womanhood? Though she loved me in her own way, my mother also hated me in a misguided way inspired by her own unhealed wounds, by her own pain, and by the confusing jealousies of general womanhood nestled in her broken heart.

When it came to my sexuality, I averted my eyes, mostly. For much of adulthood—the first twenty-five years—my sexual pleasure was typically heightened by alcohol. Sex was enjoyable, yes, but it was also tainted by my initial introduction to sex acts.

It would take years to understand that my shame was rooted in teachings that hinted at culpability on the part of females victimized in rape culture. As if something in our appearance or behavior made us victims to male prey. Ironically, women more than men tended to be the enforcers of such messages. Scorn and judgment about how we dress. Slut-shaming of women who dared to express their own version of sexual freedom. I felt all of this but had no idea what it was, had no idea what to do with it, nor did I have any idea how to extract myself from its reach.

In my drinking days, I found it difficult to enjoy sex without the high acquired by the over-consumption of alcohol. Alcohol gave me the kind of freedom I lacked when it came to appreciating my own body and experiencing the pleasurable sexual experience I'm worthy of as a human on the planet. If I was alone and wanted to pleasure myself—rub my clitoris into masturbating euphoria—I had to be drunk or tipsy. As far as I knew—based on no real information outside of church rules and the rigid social messages of my teenage years—the act of masturbation was a thing of shame. None but prostitutes, perverts, and sexual deviants chose the act of masturbation.

The thought of masturbating was just one more shameful layer to add to all the layers of shame I already felt about my existence. I was embarrassed to be in my own skin not only because I was a Black woman living in a racist society that promotes messages of Black women being hypersexual, but also because I'd already been tainted by sexual abuse in my childhood home. I didn't know yet how to accept myself as a welcome human being on the planet.

I thought everything about me was wrong—wrong childhood for its abuse, wrong gender for its routine attraction of predatory behavior, wrong skin color for its routine attraction of hatred—and I thought the wrongness was all my fault.

When I got sober ten years ago, my first order of business was to figure out how to enjoy sex without alcohol. At the time, I was too embarrassed to discuss with my husband the anxiety I felt about the eventuality of having sex without alcohol, so I kept it to myself (until the writing of this essay). However, it *does* help to be married to a hot hunk—a gorgeous Black man— who is the kindest, gentlest, and most considerate friend (among males *and* females) I've ever known. Having sex without alcohol was less challenging than I thought it would be. But sex without alcohol was still a shock to my system, and it was something I had to get used to because my moods for having sex were often unreliable and unpredictable.

I've spent all ten of my sober years (so far) relearning how to view my body in its sexual presentation. Writing (and blogging) became the patient, loving teacher which took my hand and kindly guided me through the process of relearning my own sexuality.

Among writers, I've heard it said that while a story begins with the writer, the direction the story takes often becomes an unpredictable labyrinth of fascinating turns. If anyone had told me when I decided to become a full-time writer that I would be telling the world about my body and my sexual appetites, I might have been mortified enough to abandon the writing dream and stay put in my soul-sucking day job. Right? Because I'm no sex expert. This is not a book about sex or sexual appetites. However, I *am* a sexual being and I'm done with being put in a box as a woman on the planet. I'm more than a skin complexion, more than unfortunate childhood circumstances, more than my addiction, and more than my good or bad choices.

My sexual healing became part of the story I needed to tell. Leaving it out from these essays would have made me a liar because how could I explain all the ways I felt held back from writing without offering all the ways I learned to let go? I couldn't. I followed my heart along these pages, letting the truth of my story land in its need for daylight, letting her land in sincerity.

Now that I'm here, writing about my own sexual development, I don't mind saying, I highly recommend masturbation on at least an occasionally routine basis for women of all ages. If I'm preaching to the choir, awesome! Kudos to you for being ahead of the healthy sexual expression game in womanhood. But for the women out there who may have also lost her sexual way for different reasons, I want you to know that I'm glad you're here, and it's never too late to try new things.

The inspiration for this particular essay showed up when I least expected it. And it's funny because I almost missed it due to stubbornness and the occasional know-it-all attitude I can at times exhibit as a parent (I hope writing that doesn't come back to bite me). I almost missed the inspiration to explore my sexuality more deeply because when one of my adult daughters first advised me to check out Beyonce's concert, *Homecoming*, on Netflix, I ignored the suggestion.

How could I explain to my beautiful daughter how full of self-loathing I still was? How could I admit that my throat was scratchy with self-hatred that I was still choking on after so many years of adulting? How could

I explain such a thing to her when I couldn't even admit that yet to myself? So I brushed off her suggestion initially, acting as if a Beyoncé concert on television was young people stuff. I basically told my daughter that I'd check it out one of these days in the future, maybe. I love Beyoncé and her music but since I'm not much of a concert-goer, I didn't think it was a big deal to pass on her *Homecoming* special on Netflix.

I did try to watch it initially, tuning in for all of fifteen minutes and then turning it right off.

Enough time has passed and I'm ready to be honest with myself. Watching those few minutes of *Homecoming* made me sick with jealousy, sick with envy for all the proud and beautiful Blackness on that stage. There were so many gorgeous Black women and Black men of all shapes and sizes, dressed in a wide array of bright colors and hip-hop casual styles. And then also, there was Beyoncé, brilliantly directing, standing proudly, singing songs from her smash album, *Lemonade* in her big and amazing voice, smiling brightly, living her best life. Ugh. I was so jealous of it all I couldn't see straight. I made up excuses—I don't need to see this, all those young people on that stage. Phfft! Whatevs. I already know my Black history, this is all new for them, they need this, I don't. I don't need the quotes from books I already read that they never even bothered to pick up, books by Audre Lorde, Alice Walker, and Toni Morrison. I don't need to see this.

Those young people, I thought, they're over there dancing on that stage, being all starry-eyed because they get to spend a little time with the celebrity likes of

Beyoncé and Jay-Z, like everything in Black life is one big ole party. Meanwhile, I'm still living in the REAL world, a world where messages about being Black are not as great as messages about being white. I live in a world where these kinds of racist messages have been subtly—and overtly! —hitting my brain cells since I could hold a book and turn on a television. Uh huh. I live in the real world where frustrated Black people do not always find the resolve and the energy to be starry-eyed and kind to each other.

Ugh. Oh man, I was just so *jealous*.

There was so much love radiating and bouncing between all those Black bodies. It reminded me for the millionth time of all the years of love—parental love, healthy love, community love, self-love—I'd missed out on, all the love I was still trying to get my own hands on, still trying to wrap a newly generated healthy life around, still trying to consume, still trying to cultivate, still trying to make up for in my original loss of it. The joy of those performers reminded me of the love I'd yearned for—before finally landing in a happy marriage—and the tender newness of a loving life that I was still working to solidify in order to feel more worthy as a human on the planet once and for all.

Exploring my heart around my avoidance of this particular concert, a concert easily accessible to me on Netflix, taught me an important lesson about being a victim of circumstances. Now understand, this is merely *my* truth and *my* understanding. I don't profess to speak on behalf of other victims. I understand that there are stages of victimization, just like there are stages of grief, and everyone experiences their victimization differently. I'm speaking for myself here.

It occurred to me that because I was hurt by my victimization, having been victimized by childhood circumstances as well as discriminatory—racist—circumstances repeatedly throughout my life, I'd gotten into the habit of expecting the worst. In those instances, when I expected the worst, I'd strike against myself preemptively, creating disappointment before disappointment found me first. When I saw the opportunity to view a concert that I might actually enjoy, I made up excuses to not watch it. In this way, I could hold on to some heartbreak about my tendency to feel left out in the world, hold on to despair as a form of protection against getting my hopes up over a potentially enjoyable event. Despite lived proof that life can be exciting and fun at different turns, as a former victim accustomed to disappointment, my almost knee-jerk response to the concert was to pass, dismissing it as something for the younger crowd.

I forgot all about the concert for an entire year.

One day, while on break from writing this book, I was eating a late lunch with my laptop before me on the kitchen table. I'd been done writing for the day and I wanted something mindless to watch, so I clicked on Netflix. I was clicking through random titles of movies, standup comedy, concerts—oh yeah, there it was again: *Homecoming*. I sighed and said, what the hell.

Maybe what happened next, the feelings which flooded my body, happened because there was no longer anyone asking me to watch it. Maybe it was because I was alone at home, tired, bored, and had no more expectations for what remained of my workday. Maybe it was simply my time to be open to a new revelation about Black womanhood. Maybe it was any combination and all of those things put together.

As I watched the opening of *Homecoming*, it was as if I was seeing it for the first time. How had I missed all this splendor on one stage when viewing it initially the year before? I saw dozens of Black females in a rainbow of Black complexions and I was newly transfixed. My heart raced, my skin tingled, and I could not stop gaping. The concert began with a Black female marching band leader, tap-tap-tapping furiously on a drum strapped to her chest, with a deepening scowl on her face. Seconds after finishing her solo intro, she blew loudly on a whistle, and out marched Beyoncé in a sequined bodysuit and cape, flanked by her entourage of Black women dressed in one-legged catsuits with painted-on Nefertiti images. Something at my core vibrated like a dog hearing its special whistle.

Of course, I'd seen concerts—though none like this—on television before. I've seen women sing at mikes onstage and backup singers swaying behind them. I've seen videos where lead singers perform choreographed routines with numerous dancers around them. I'd been moved by musical numbers before. But this was different.

It was different because there were *so many* Black bodies on one stage. And there were frequent nods and odes to Black culture: Black history, Black college traditions, and Black power saluting. Gone were my jealous pangs of feeling excluded, excluded from the general mainstream of whiteness *and* the seemingly exclusive unity of Blackness.

There on the small computer screen, in the space of my own kitchen, my feelings of unbelonging were supplanted by the power of self-determined, self-defined BLACK FEMALE SEXUALITY. What in the name of sex-kittens-turned-cheetahs-twerking shenanigans was this beautiful display before me? I felt my hips twitching! I felt a screamy kind of hysterical laughter bubbling up in my throat, like I would throw my head back and cackle delightedly. I hit the pause button and grabbed my Bluetooth speaker, pumping the volume all the way up. I abandoned my lunch and proceeded to dance to every song as I watched the concert in my kitchen.

All those Black women looked like *me* or someone related to me. Their bodies were a multitude of differing shapes and sizes, large and curvy, short and tall, thin and wide, lithe and muscular. Every one of those Black women on that stage shook their butts and ground their hips like it was their proudest and most exhilarating moment, like it was the last thing they'd been given to do in life, and they meant to give it everything they had. I saw a wink in the skinfolds of their smiles and snarls, a wink that let me know it was okay to be my sexual self, after all. I giggled, looking around the kitchen, imagining a neighbor spying through the window and witnessing me as someone losing her mind because I was dancing all alone to loud music. I didn't let that thought stop me, I kept dancing and grinning. I watched

Homecoming three more times that week, once with my husband and twice more by myself.

After my third viewing, I decided to spend more time naked. It was the first time I'd ever spent extended stretches of time in the nude. Why, I asked myself, had I spent so many years feeling the need to be covered? Since my teenage years, I'd been in the habit of dressing quickly after showers. I did this for so long, I never stopped to notice how strange it was. Even when I lived alone in my own apartments. Even after I got married. Nakedness had always been directly linked with shame and shameful feelings in my mind. I forgot to get over that. I forgot that once I'd grown up and was out in the world, on my own, I could completely live life any way I chose. Obviously, I did *some* of that. I'd enjoyed my own autonomy, did whatever I wanted to do. I'd done my share of partying, lived some of life on the wild side—alcohol-induced, but still. I traveled too and made homes for myself in different cities. But a human life is so layered and we're all so complex in our nuances. I forgot to return to the embrace of my own naked body and my natural sexuality.

I rediscovered masturbation. I sure did. It had been way too many years (probably since I stopped drinking ten years ago) since the last time I masturbated.

Besides tasks like writing, errands, and bill paying, I decided it was time to put masturbation on the to-do list. Why the hell not? Masturbating is as mood-enhancing and life-giving as any other physical and recreational outlet. Why aren't women talking about this with each other more? We need to discuss, ladies.

There are all these acceptable phrases for male masturbation—jerk off, wank, beat the meat, choke the chicken—which suggests that male masturbation is seen as the most natural thing in the world. Meanwhile, what terms do women have for masturbating? Exactly.

Watching *Homecoming* woke me up. It reminded me of the feeling I used to get as a younger woman in crowded, dimly lit dance clubs, filled with mostly Black people, where the music from the speakers boomed so loudly, you felt the rhythm vibrating in your chest. Most of us would be high on alcohol, weed—and likely other drugs that I was too chickenshit to get into—and the euphoria of dancing together, bodies pressed together due to limited space. And we'd dance like we were all possessed, as if all our movements—swinging arms, shaking heads, bending knees, and gyrating hips—were a matter of life or death, sweating profusely with soaked through shirts, skirts, jeans, you name it, all apparel would be damp or wet. Every now and then we'd glance away from our dancing partner and laughingly catch the eye of another person—male or female—and we'd smile widely in appreciation, as if to say, Yasss! I see you! I feel you! We belong to all this wild fun right now, baby!

It was like a secret language that brought joy to our hearts like fellow revelers in a parade. We felt the rare and exotic blessings of solidarity and approval so keenly missing from the light of day in daily lives as Black people in America. And so, we danced into the night as hard as possible, knowing it would come to an end at last call.

As I woke to my nearly forgotten sexuality, I was reminded of my Black female ancestry, reminded of the way African women were brought with their men across an ocean, and made to stand naked on auctioning blocks. I recalled the history of our shared humiliation and shame—as Black women and Black men—about our naked bodies because the eyes of white slave-traders gawked at our foremothers with a combination of disgust, greed, hatred, and lust.

When, after a few hundred years of fighting and bloodshed, Black people gained their freedom and—some semblance of—protection under American laws, we descendants continued to carry the remnants of slavery's traumas in our bloodlines, in the fabric of our DNA. And yet, we continued to press forward, finding levels of improvement for our lives, some of us finding more wealth than we dreamed possible, some of us continuing to dangle beneath poverty's line, many more of us landing somewhere in between.

Between my Black history—having to unearth so much of what was never taught about it in my home or at school—and the lived individual experiences of my own life, I got lost and therefore, lost track of the sexuality which should have been mine by birthright. I can only imagine how strange it is for some of my loved ones to read my explicit musings on sex and masturbation. But to me, what I am saying here is as overdue and no less logical than trying to figure out where the heck I put my car keys, retracing steps to find them, so that I can make it out of the house in time for the next appointment.

The patriarchy has already stolen so much from me as a Black woman—stolen so much from *all* of us in one way or another—I'm ready to reclaim myself before I die. This means I choose to walk around naked in my home as much as possible. This also means forgoing panties I no longer care to wear all the time under clothing. This means I will masturbate with delicious abandon as much as I like during daylight hours.

I've taken my body back and I am no longer dragging myself along the ground of life like an injured animal, under the heavy burden of shame. Fuck shame. I'm a sexy AF Black woman routinely enjoying sex in unprecedented ways with her very lucky husband. Oh, yes! I'm fortunate to be married to a husband who's always adored me and made me feel appreciated. But now? Howard is looking at me like, *Who are you and what did you do with my wife?* He's looking at me like I'm the gift he gets to open, only to be surprised by a more extraordinary gift than the one he thought he already had.

This is what Sexual Healing looks like. I got naked; I found my clitoris. I feel powerful, mighty, and unstoppable. I am woman, hear me roar!

15

FROM ZERO TO HERO WITH CONFIDENCE

I'm just a woman, telling her story. I may roar on occasions—when I need to—but I'm not in perpetual roaring mode. The truth is, I have just as much fear as the next person. Clearly, I'm living the kind of life these days where I'm less intimidated by Fear than I used to be. But believe me, fear does still show up and can still overwhelm me at times if I let it. I have to make the effort to work at actively keeping my fears in check.

Everyone lives with fear. It's an emotion just like any other and when used correctly, it protects us, feeding instinctual choices. But it does take practice to avoid being consumed by fear.

Depending on who we are, the fears we harbor the most can be exacerbated by witnessing violence incited by racial tyranny, misogyny, or homophobia. For many of us, these vulnerable positions in the patriarchy cause our lives and self-identifying issues to intersect. In other words, we share common bonds of discrimination.

In our human family we're each frequently making choices which can be rooted in the intersecting

142

discrimination factors. It's fascinating to notice how many of us experience our separate struggles in isolation because life has exhausted us to the point where we no longer want to be bothered. Stay out of my lane and I'll stay out of yours.

Not everyone wants to be seen. Some of us prefer to keep our heads down as a method of preservation. Most of us are living ordinary, anonymous lives. We don't always pay attention to the common bonds of difficulties that might bring us closer together.

And when you don't see a version of your own story anywhere, you tend to feel invisible (which is oftentimes, the whole point). Getting older is what made me finally say, enough, I refuse to go on living this way anymore. I refuse to die, trapped in mental despair with feelings like fear, sadness, and anger.

The existence of this book probably makes me look confident. True. But I did it afraid. I felt the fear and wrote it anyway.

Despite the appearance of taking a stand to be seen, it isn't always because I'm brimming with confidence. Sometimes it's simply because I'm fed up or I'm tired or I'm hangry (as in, hungry and angry). Sometimes it's because I'm having a good moment and I feel hopeful enough to desire connection with other humans who feel hopeful too.

The truth also is this—my naivete has brought me here, to this book writing place. I didn't think about all the fear that might be involved in a soul-bearing kind of book. What I thought about was all the frustrated Black women like me, who're stifling their potential, all the

Black women who've gotten fed up and hyper-distrustful of The World in general and of each other as a result. And rather than give up, I chose to keep going, writing my way through to answers, sharing with other hopefuls exactly how I got it done in the hope of starting a story-sharing revolution (I know! Maybe it sounds crazy. But a lot of revolutionary shit in history sounded crazy before it got done).

I wrote my way from fear to courage to confidence by saying, *what if.* What if I go first with my own story? What if a Black person wrote a different kind of memoir? Because oh my god, look at all the amazing books by Black people already out here. Look at how far Black people have come in the literary world. How exciting for us that we get to explore so many different kinds of stories where we get to see ourselves! But what if there are more versions yet to be told? What if I wrote something a little more vulnerable? What if I trusted the world to meet me where I am with my own experiences?

I used to be clueless and hapless. As alcoholic living gradually drifted into the rearview mirror of life, and as this brain of mine started drying out, newly clarified thinking revealed the truth of who I really was.

A few years after I got sober, I chose several friends to confide in about the extremely low opinion I'd held about myself for so many years, how in my heart I honestly believed I was beneath most people, and how I never felt worthy of anyone's time. These were friends who'd known me for years, who saw the more loose and wilder side of me. When I describe what happened next, what the responses were, I'm not doing it to insult anyone. There's no shade intended at all. I'm simply making a point due to the similarity in responses. Each person appeared shocked—and a little disappointed—like they couldn't believe what I was saying. And because I was unprepared for their disbelief, I didn't know where to go next with my thinking—or where to go next with the conversation—on the subject of confidence.

This is what can happen when we aren't being true to ourselves, when we're pretending to be things we're not. I didn't have a plan for how to unmask.

In the *working-me* mask, it appeared I loved a job populated with people whose behavior often filled me with rage. In the *agreeable-me* mask, it appeared that I was ingratiating and self-deprecating ninety-five percent of the time when all the while, my inner-child felt perpetually ignored and abandoned. I'd finally gotten to the point (in middle-age) where I realized I needed to pay more attention to her, the little girl on the inside, listen to her more, allow her to breathe instead of continuing to stifle her as I hid *real* me from the outside world.

Behind the mask, whenever someone close to me insulted me subtly, giving me what's known as a harmless slight or dig, most of the time I pretended my feelings weren't hurt even when I found the remark quite painful. I did a lot of smiling, acting as if I was fine all the time, no matter what was being said or what action was unfolding, when underneath the fake grin, I wasn't fine at all.

We grow through seasons, convinced that we've outgrown every stretch of fabric from our past. We pack it all up in sealed boxes and we move forward. That's what I did. I honestly never thought there would ever come a need for me to pull down those mental boxes and unpack any of the contents. I packed up my childhood confusion about the abuse and lack of love without realizing confusion was still underneath every thought, choice, and word spoken in my active life.

How do you stop the world from its constant propulsion and swift momentum as you try to belong? I couldn't do it. I couldn't raise my hand in front of people and say, I have absolutely no idea what you're talking about or, I have no idea what that even means. I couldn't join the conversation by leading with, you're being really mean right now and I'm not sure if it's me or if this is just the way things go, if this is the way we're all expected to talk to each other, but this is really hurting my feelings. Right? Picture an adult saying all that. It's just not done.

While I was busy acting *as if* to fit in, not only was I painting myself into a corner, I was also inviting reinjuries from others around me.

I didn't know how to get out of the mask-wearing after doing it for so long. I guess I knew at some point, *eventually*, I'd have to stop with mask-wearing because I wouldn't be able to keep it up. It took too much energy to sustain and I was tiring more easily with age.

Well, *Eventually* came knocking in the form of book writing. And it wasn't a quiet knock, it was more like a pounding fist on the door. Eventually said: *You want this dream? You want to be able to write a book? You want to be able to look people in the eye and ask them to trust you with their stories? Well, you're going to have to take off the fucking mask. You're going to have to tell the truth, telling the story of you first. Because the roads you've been bumping along on—acting as if, sneaking peaks and taking cues from the world in absence of parental guidance—has repeatedly brought you to dead ends. Until you start telling the truth, you're going to keep hitting walls.*

The truth is, I've been clueless at repeated turns throughout the years and made to feel embarrassed about my cluelessness. I didn't know where the answers were or how to ask for help because I didn't want to appear as someone who didn't know what she was doing. I didn't want to show my cards, let others know that I might be struggling after living all these years as a grownup. I'm well aware that I'm an adult and that sooner or later, we're all expected to step fully into our grownup bodies and bear responsibility for whatever adulting brings our way.

I've done this, stepped into responsibilities fully, but not without occasionally destroying entire portions of my life, blowing shit into smithereens by way of hapless choices, and losing time with having to rebuild before I could continue forward. Or losing time, living in unhealthy conditions—burnt-out shells of dysfunctional thinking, mental dwelling places I didn't know were toxic, killing me slowly over time—because it had become a matter of survival, going to work, paying bills, and caring for family. I thought it was impossible to stop and evaluate the mess I was making and clean it up.

I wore the masks and I built walls around my heart for protection, walls layered with anger and sadness, walls layered with all my years of wounding and all my years of hurt. I toughened up, developed a thick skin—which wasn't as thick as I hoped it would be, but still—because I was intent on protecting myself from the possibility of new hurts and disappointments. This worked for me in most instances but sometimes—when I let my guard down on days when I was feeling extra lonely or nostalgic or hungry or whatever—it didn't work, and I'd suffer reinjury all over again. I'd then reinforce the walls with fresh layers of added anger, added sadness, sprinkling a little extra rage to scare off potential offenders.

These walls around my heart kept me clueless and hapless. I've been extremely lucky in friendships, finding women along life's way who were generous, nurturing, and loyal. Those were the friends who I cooked with, friends who I exchanged funny stories with, friends who I drank with and laughed with, friends who babysat for me when I was a financially struggling single-parent, friends who let me cry with them after a bad breakup, and friends who would have given me anything I needed.

However, when I was young and dumb, those weren't the only kind of friends I had. Through more periods than I care to admit, I used to also be a follower who sometimes fell in with the wrong crowd—even when I wasn't so young. I used to be *that* woman, the woman who didn't realize when she was being tricked or hustled or didn't realize right away when the joke she didn't get was about *her*.

I wasn't always good at figuring people out, differentiating between those who honestly cared about me from those who just wanted to take advantage of me. This is how it goes down when your generosity is inspired by a deep-seated need to be liked, loved, or accepted.

Turns out—now that I'm older, wiser, and privy to more kinds of stories than my own—this is the way it happened for a lot of women. As women, we tend to lead with our hearts first. We get burned and then we learn. Well, I didn't learn as quickly as your average woman.

Now I can talk about this because these events are behind me and I've wizened up. But when I was living through all these episodes of my own cluelessness, I felt completely devastated and powerless. It wasn't just choosing the wrong kinds of friends. There were also plenty of legitimate businesses that preyed on my naivete—realtor companies, predatory lending institutions, car dealers, utility bill collectors, landlords, and more.

Here's what I will no longer dismiss myself by saying: *this happens to everybody*. Because depending on skin color, gender, sexual orientation, and/or any combination thereof, it most certainly does *not* happen to everybody in the *same* way.

I finally understand how deep our social programming goes. I may have even said the *everybody experiences this* phrase in some places in the book. Hopefully, I remembered to put the phrase in a context that shows that I'm trying to change the way I think and see the world after so much brainwashing by patriarchy messages. Depending on who we are in the hierarchy of privileged American life, we experience life episodes differently. I had to grow up more as an adult and become more self-aware, healing old wounds, to understand this properly.

I still cringe when I think of all those times I was dismissive about one or another of my daughters' feelings at times when they were trying to explain something they were going through. But because I hadn't yet figured out my own life, I didn't yet have the patience or the correct answers to fully help or reassure them. Instead, sometimes I went to the knee-jerk default so many of us resort to thanks to socialized propaganda, saying—everyone goes through this or it could be worse or you're not the only one. All of these things are completely unhelpful and possibly damaging when someone is trying to get a crater off their chest. Sometimes we just need to be heard and that's all. And in being heard, we don't need to be dismissed with phrases that remind us how insignificant our problems are just because we number in the billions among humans and everyone is supposedly going through similar experiences that we're going through. Let's stop saying that bullshit to each other because it's not true.

But I digress.

How did I go from zero to hero in my own story? How did I shrug off the bravado and put on real confidence?

I fell in love with myself.

Yep. I went ahead and did exactly the thing that The World specifically told us, through all its shaming tools—of memes, blogs, op-ed pieces, movies, books, tv shows, neighbors, well-meaning friends, and numerous other talking humans—not to do: I fell in love with the sound of my own voice. I fell head over heels in love with my Self. Gasp! I know!

Disgusting.

Who does that? What kind of person falls in love with herself? Society's outlook on people who love themselves—celebrities, for instance—isn't good at all. We're taught, people like that are the bane of our existence (unless they're entertaining us or crashing and burning into train-wreck glory, which in that case, is cool and acceptable). We're supposed to be reviled by people like that.

I had to fall in love with myself as a way to begin to thrive, as a way to heft a dream onto my own shoulders and stand all the way up for myself in the most loving way for once (and repeatedly). I had to become my own mom and my own dad. I had to redirect my focus, turning within. I became my own hero. Yes, it felt weird and awkward at first. But I learned to gush and swoon at my own reflection the way a mother without demons might have done for me when I was five or when I was nine or when I was nineteen. Why? Because I'm a human being and it is what I deserve. It's what we *all* deserve.

Go ahead. Try it. Fall in love with yourself and watch your entire world open up like an exotic flower turning its petals gratefully to a beaming sun.

Even if you had the benefit of loving parents, even if you have more privilege than the next person, Love can never be exhausted. As I've explained about my findings on the love-journey, the more love I have for myself, the easier it is for me to show love to other people, even the annoying ones on the planet.

Cultivating courage and confidence didn't happen overnight. It takes time and patience, not much different from the investment made in becoming lovers or friends or parents to each other as human beings. There's going to be a learning curve, a slow period of figuring out your own needs. Courting myself, doing extra loving things felt strange and uncomfortable in the beginning. Besides when brushing my teeth, doing my hair, and trying on outfits, I never really paid too much attention to my image in the mirror. But I learned how to stay put, stared into my own eyes, really looked at my face, and gazed at my naked body. It's illogical that we'd shrink from our own image and still expect other people to look upon us with love and treat us with love, especially when it comes to intimacy.

I highly recommend all or any combination of the following—in no particular order—to incorporate into daily routines as a way to begin activating deliberate acts of self-love:

- Mirror-talk
- Meditation
- Journaling
- Audio journaling
- Video journaling
- Masturbation

Self-hate sounds like a severe and drastic way to describe what I was doing to myself with all the years of mask-wearing, but it's the truth. For a long time, I wanted *out* of my skin and I wanted *out* of my gender. I wanted out of everything that was associated with the truth of every experience I'd ever lived through. I didn't want to be the person who'd lived my kind of life. After following as many of The World's rules as I could, seeing how the act of following murdered my soul in steady increments, I decided to try a different tack called truth-telling. It's not that I've given up on the world. The world is actually still beautiful in all its raw ugliness and beauty, in all the conflicting ways it evolves, carrying us forward. I don't hate this world. On the contrary, I believe so much in what's possible for our shared humanity, that I'm willing to do whatever it takes to make our world a better place, even if that makes me look like a vulnerable, crazy person cutting completely against the grain. Even if it looks like I'm standing totally alone with my ideas—which I know I'm not. I'm standing all the way up with my voice to say I now know The World needs me—it needs all of us! —and I matter.

I'm not inventing the wheel over here, I'm simply doing life differently, moving beyond surviving to become someone who thrives.

16

RENAMING MYSELF MIA

Most of the people who know me in real life know me as *Maria*. The name of my last blog was, *On Becoming Maria*. However, according to the byline of this book, I'm now calling myself *Mia*.

Yeah, about that ….

By choosing this name for the byline, I wasn't trying to hide from the people who knew me as *Maria*, although it may look like that. I'm done with all that hiding and mask-wearing stuff. I decided, in keeping with all the positive changes I've made for myself—especially as a woman who intentionally moved from self-hating to self-loving—it was time to let *Maria* go.

I never liked my name, *Maria*, when I was a little girl. I was confused by it.

Maria is a popular female name, often found in Spanish-speaking countries. I have no beef with Latinx culture, especially since Latinx is a part of my heritage. But in my family, our lineage is populated by more African ancestry than Latin ancestry. Why, I'd often wonder, did my parents name me *Maria*? Especially when all throughout childhood, everyone in the family called me by a different name. Without context or explanation, my parents, siblings, and cousins had always called me *Angie*. I was confused whenever someone—like my grandmother, for example—called me *Maria*.

I thought I was going to spend the rest of life luxuriating under the moniker of *Angie* until the day a teacher burst my bubble in the early days of a new school year.

I was an immigrant child, still new to the American public school system. I was in unchartered adult waters now, completely foreign territory, where all of the teachers were white. My teacher, Mrs. S, had had enough of the conflicting names I was going by and she cornered me one morning as we all streamed into the classroom, finding our assigned seats like little soldiers. I thought I was in trouble. I'd only been in the first grade a few days and I didn't know Mrs. S very well yet. All I knew so far was she looked older than my kindergarten teacher and she smiled way less. Mrs. S was a slender woman who wore straight, belted dark skirts and floral print, buttoned-up, polyester blouses with wide collars. Her wrinkled skin seemed incongruous with her hair, a dark brown, bouffant wig, shaped like a football helmet. Seeing how terrified I was to be singled out, Mrs. S smiled broadly, and I exhaled, feeling a bit of relief. Especially seeing the way her calm eyes locked on my wide, stunned eyes and held them as she talked.

I was pleasantly surprised to hear sincere concern in the syrup of her voice as she inquired about my two names. When I explained that all of my family and friends called me *Angie*, Mrs. S asked which name I preferred. In that moment, I felt the urge to grab Mrs. S around her narrow hips with my skinny little arms and squeeze. But I kept my arms at my side, not wanting to appear too eager. I never imagined this moment could be a possibility: a grownup desiring my opinion, inviting me to weigh in. I smiled and told her, *Angie*. Mrs. S smiled and hesitated. After a brief silence she said, *Well, since Maria is the name on all your school records, why don't we go with that instead.* It wasn't a question or a request. I nodded dumbly and found my seat among the rest of the class.

I learned to live with *Maria* only because public school records trumped family nicknames. I ended up having a different teacher in the second grade who never even thought to ask me about my conflicting names because by then, the name *Angie* had disappeared from the mouths of all my classmates. But the interaction with Mrs. S left its mark; I wanted to know where my name came from.

At home, I was allowed to be *Angie* but in school, I was forced to be *Maria*. Why? So I did the unthinkable. I asked my mother what the deal was with my name. This was the beginning of me setting myself apart from my siblings, asking too many questions of adults.

In the home I grew up in, children were to be seen and not heard. Under very few circumstances were we allowed to question adults, even if the question was logical, even if the question was necessary for our progress. I learned early to distinguish what was considered—primarily in black communities—white people's behavior from black people's behavior in our home. It wasn't even broken down for us as kids; there were no verbal explanations. All it took was a look from my mother like, don't even *think* about it. This is *not* television. You *will* be whipped. Do *not* ask me any questions. It was considered rude and disrespectful to question an adult. What can I say? It was a different time in Black culture. The youth of my generation was raised on old school principals. The grownup world was distinctly separate and mysterious from the child world.

This was also the beginning of clowning for me as a survival method at home, using humor to lighten moods and disarm. It usually worked, even on typically grumpy adults. Putting on my best clown face, wearing a wide, open-mouth smile like I was in the midst of laughing, I asked my mother the question. *How did I get the name Maria?* At first, I got the mother-look, but seeing my goofy smile, my mother relaxed and told me the story.

Turns out, my grandmother named me.

My mother already had a name picked out for her first-born daughter (me), but her relationship with my father was shaky and she wanted to do something she knew would please him. My father had a name in mind too, one suggested to him by his Cuban mother. The two women didn't like each other. And yet, my mother was too smitten with my father to withhold her gesture of compliance, so she conceded, accepted the Cuban inspired name for her Jamaican-born baby.

However, in a bid to also preserve her position—as in, no one tells me what to call my own child—she defiantly and pointedly ignored the name she permitted on the birth certificate, calling me *Angie* instead. *Angie* is the only name my mother has ever called me.

I used to think this was a very cool story. Or rather, I perceived it as a cool story when I was a kid. It was a way of feeling loved, convincing myself that these two women loved me so much, they went to battle, fighting over the honor of naming me. Secretly, I was rooting for my mother though, because *Angie* was the only name I'd known up to that point. They both won. However, officially—in places where documents were relied upon for grades, bill payment, salary compensation, and filing taxes—my name has always been *Maria*.

I've let go of the fantasy I once had of being fought over by two matriarchs. The fight was nothing more than a power struggle between two women over the attention of one man. Family wouldn't be family if they didn't come with their share of drama. Now that I've come through it and I'm standing on the other side, the drama has become my writing fodder. Lucky for me, it's the stuff you *can't* make up that provides material for the best stories.

The way I see it nowadays is, a long time ago, my mother was a young woman, in love with my father. I imagine she had dreams just like we all do when we're young and full of hope. I bet she was thrilled to give birth to a daughter, someone she hoped to raise in the happily ever after glow of marital bliss. Having lived so many impoverished years on an island of incongruent beauty, life in America seemed like the land of promises and possibilities. Unfortunately, when we move forward, whoever we are—whatever has shaped us—will move right along with us. My parents were in for a rude awakening. Their past may have been messy, but America wasn't going to be the wonderland so many immigrants thought of it as. I had a similar journey of reawakening, which is the way life can go with generational cycles.

I love my parents. And I'm thankful for the life they gave me, no matter how difficult the time spent between us was. But I am not my parents. Nor am I merely our legacy of pain. I'm more than those shared sad experiences.

So as the book publishing date approached, I wanted to step into the world as the woman who'd finally learned to embrace everything about who she is, the woman who'd finally learned how to love her Self. I wanted to step into the world as the woman who'd stopped the generational cycle of self-hatred.

I used the acronym of my initials—*Maria E. Archer*—and got Mia. The H is a private name I've given myself. I consider H a name too sacred to share publicly because H is my most cherished and revered side of self. H is (future) elderly me. Whenever I'm feeling at my lowest, saddest, and most hopeless, I turn to H, journaling to her about my angst, and writing to her (imagining an older, wiser woman who loves me and knows me well) always makes me feel better. As a writer, living her best life these days, I now call myself *Mia H. Archer*.

Does this mean that loved ones are forbidden to call me *Maria* or forbidden to call me *Angie*? No. I don't mind continuing to be called by any of the names I've always been known by. Besides, now that I'm older, I consider myself fortunate to have been given two really beautiful names—Angie *and* Maria.

As I went through transformations in the growing up process, I wasn't always so grateful in the names department.

I did go through a season some years ago, when I was frustrated and angry, when I hadn't fully dealt with all the wounding. Not my most shining moments. During that stretch of time, I angrily declared a moratorium on the name *Angie*. And my poor startled friends obliged me as best they could, trying mightily to remember. All I'd offered as an explanation back then was, *Maria* is the name written on my birth certificate. What I didn't say was, my mother broke my heart and spent our ensuing years together—once I became an adult—adding salt to wounds with cruel commentary, and I don't know how to stop being mad at her.

Well, I'm not mad at my mother anymore. I'm not angry with either of my parents anymore. For me, it's not so much about forgiveness as it is about moving on and letting go. I used to think I needed them to apologize and make amends to me for all the pain they caused. But when I asked and saw that they had no idea how to become the kind of people who could do this—it took some years, but I got there—I had to let it go. I had to let them be who they came here to be. We're not pals. My parents and I eventually parted ways to live separate lives. But they and I get to live our lives in peace. Families come in all shapes, sizes, and endings. There is no right or wrong way to be a family. It's whatever makes us feel safe and feel loved. My parents broke up and got back together with each other. In their own way, I think they finally found love.

Don't misunderstand me, I'm not positing myself as some paragon of virtue in the forgiveness department. No way. I'm not anyone's model to follow as an example of how to deal with parents who hurt them. I'm doing the best I can with the cards I was dealt. I still have rough days, days when I feel sad and lost, days when I'm disappointed that my parents gave up so easily. It's like living with grief. You learn to manage and live with it.

The longer I live, the more joy and love I find in life, the less of those days I experience. I feel fortunate to have led this kind of life so far. Love has found me in surprising, splendid and plentiful ways.

Underneath all the names, I'm simply a girl who fought her demons to be here—Angie, Maria, Mia. I'm all these selves and so much more. You can call me by whichever name brings us closer as humans. Because at the end of the day, what I believe is this: we're all angels on Earth, merely walking each other home.

~ Mia ~

17

FRIENDS WHO HAPPEN TO BE WHITE

While conducting research for the Black women's friendship book, I met a significant number of Black women who asked why I wasn't writing about female friendships among *everyone* instead of focusing solely on Black people. Those women would go on to say that female friendships share universal traits.

Uh huh. Then I would stifle my eye-rolls, thinking, *Really? Do I **look** like Oprah with a team of staff members?* Each time I was asked, I'd politely explain, this is my first book and I'm only one person. I don't have the resources to cover—delving into research about—all the different races of people living among us. In the explanation I would also add, as a Black woman, I felt it was important to write a book that was strictly about us. We *deserve* to have such a book written. The asking person would nod in understanding.

But I get it. I understand we're living in different times as Black people. The division of color lines is less strict and deadly (police killings notwithstanding) than they were say, fifty years ago. These days, some of us belong to interracial families. Some of us grew up in all-white or interracial neighborhoods. Some of us have white people in our lives who are extremely dear to us. Despite its history of racism and racial terror, America is still home to individuals of all colors who aren't perpetrators of racist acts or (necessarily, always) victims of racist assaults. Ok, that last thing obviously varies depending on your neighborhood and other intersecting identifiers. But overall, America—despite all her racial complexities—is our home and we do still love her.

With that said and in keeping with the larger pieces of the story that brought me here, I need to talk about how significantly my life was impacted by the relationships I've had with white people. This feels huge for me as I look back from my position in the year 2020 because it's been so painful in general, but also so viciously wounding to Blacks in particular.

If it weren't for the extraordinary friendships I shared with some of the Caucasians I knew as a young adult in the 1990s, after the stunning turn of political events of 2016, and the devastating number of killings of Blacks by white police officers in recent decades, I'm almost certain I would feel an irrational hatred towards white people.

Everything happens for a reason. I believe this completely. Nothing is arbitrary in the universe. Even having a racist misogynist for a president has served a purpose, shaking many of us out of the collective feelings of malaise and apathy which has touched so many areas of all our lives, inspiring us to become more acutely aware of our positions, drawing us into more united fronts as challengers of an oppressive social order. I wouldn't describe myself necessarily as a member of the "woke" members of our collective, but I am definitely more awake than I've ever been.

As I reflect, it's clear to me that I was supposed to meet the angels who were placed directly on my path during those 1990 years. I never thought I'd say this, but I miss those years. And while I don't wish to have them back, I do wish I'd shown more appreciation for that time in my life. I do wish I'd kept phone numbers and addresses of some of the beautiful people I used to know.

What I've come to learn is, it's hard to know while you're actively existing through a particular period how that season will fare, how it will line up against past and future seasons. We're usually too busy looking ahead or behind us to notice and truly appreciate how good our current moments are. If we're lucky, we get random, fleeting moments of awareness, and we remember to smile or laugh longer because we noticed.

As for me, in those days, I wasn't paying attention. I was still a novice when it came to emotional self-management, often struggling with my depression. When I got down in the dumps back then, it felt like those sad days largely outnumbered the contented and joyful days. What I know now is, perspective changes things. It's less about how the number of good and bad days compare and more about which days I keep my focus on as I live through them.

I was still growing up back then.

From childhood straight through college graduation, all of my closest circles of friends were comprised of Black people. I wasn't deliberately trying to stay away from relationships with whites, it was just a matter of spending time with people I felt the most at home and comfortable with. I *did* have casual acquaintances and casual friendships with whites whom I'd met in college. I briefly kept in contact with two journalism classmates who happen to be white, but once I got married, we lost touch.

During senior year of college, I drifted away from pretty much all of my peers because I'd spent that year living with my boyfriend and getting pregnant with our first child. Immediately after college graduation, I landed fully into the grownup world of motherhood, marriage, and work. My social life came screeching to a dramatic halt. By the time I realized that childhood and college friends had drifted out of sight—it was actually me who drifted, being young and lacking in social skills which might have helped me bridge the lifestyle divides between us—I was living in Upstate New York, surrounded by mostly white people.

Even though I was in my twenties, I still didn't have enough actual experiences with white people to possess an informed opinion about them yet. My pre-college impression of whites came mostly from television, second-hand stories told by other Blacks, and general social rules dictated by the ubiquitous media. Racism, with its seeming octopus arms in constant motion, slamming into nearly all things American culture, had merely brushed itself, feather-like, against my life by that point. What I saw as minor discriminating behaviors in random mall stores and occasional apartment searches were what I'd come to expect as a Black person living in America.

My first real lesson on racial awareness came while I was in middle school, when I watched the television movie, *Roots,* based on the book by Alex Haley. That was my first real understanding of American slavery and white hatred against Blacks.

The second orientation to racial awareness came less than five years later, while on winter break from college, visiting home. For several days our televisions were tuned in to the Howard Beach story. (On December 20, 1986, a Black man was murdered and another was severely beaten in Howard Beach, Queens, New York in a racially charged attack which heightened racial tensions in New York City.)

And yet, each of these events—seeing *Roots* and following the news about the Howard Beach murder— happened in such relative distance from my life, it felt almost like a bad dream. There were no guiding adults in my youth willing to (or able to properly) ground the reality of each event with my life, to help me feel the connectedness of my own Blackness. When my parents did make comments of frustrated anger about these hateful acts, it was either to themselves, speaking out loud to no one in particular, or to each other. The awkwardness between them and I stood as a barrier to any heart-to-heart opportunities on racial matters affecting Black people.

As far as I knew, discrimination was the way of life for Blacks in America. That I had been subjected to mild discrimination based on skin color on some occasions, far and few between, didn't faze me enough to dwell on. I had bigger fish to fry. I was more focused on my mental health or lack thereof. My life thus far had already been a traumatizing train wreck. After the childhood I managed to live through, racism was the least of my concerns.

As a married working mother, I found myself getting to know white people for the first time in the office where I worked. Most of us were still young enough and unseasoned enough to be open to learning from each other. Racial tension wasn't hanging over our 1990s workplace like the cloud that it became for me and others twenty years later.

I was a social worker in a fledgling agency that existed offsite from three umbrella agencies that employed each of us. I didn't know about social work organizations back then, but I knew enough to know that our agency's name was the most unimaginative title anyone of us had ever heard of. The sign on the door leading to our offices said, *The Case Management Team*. The CMT acronym appeared on all of our reports, letterhead, and other official documents.

Our job was to provide services to at-risk youth— youth from economically depressed neighborhoods, in danger of falling through the cracks of the social and school system—through one-on-one counseling, motivational talks to groups in community centers, and talks to those assembled in the local prison (for youth with minor offenses who were about to return to society). We also provided instructions to teachers and medical professionals on how to identify at-risk youth and work with them. We were all college graduates, some with social work degrees and others, like me, with on the job training courses provided by the umbrella agency we worked for.

There were two to three of us from each of the larger agencies—a hospital, a mental health facility, and a large clinic—which employed us. Together, like so many eager do-gooders before us, we fully believed that we were going to change the world. We loved our jobs. The office culture was laid back because all the truly senior people—the managers and executives—were offsite, at the headquarter locations. The onsite CMT supervisor, Millicent (not her real name), was just one year out of social work graduate school. As an MSW, it was her job to oversee our work and guide us in providing services and outreach to the community.

This was my second real grownup job, meaning it was the second post-college job I had which lasted more than one year. Millicent was my first experience with a super-cool white person. She looked like a hippie—straight blonde hair which she often wore loose, hanging to the base of her spine. She smiled easily and had the kind of warm personality which made whoever she was talking to feel welcome. On sunny, summer days Millicent sometimes held our staff meetings at a nearby park, where we'd sit in circle, and take turns updating each other on client statuses. It was Millicent who initiated our monthly after-work get-togethers for Happy Hours at the local bars.

We didn't always get along. Just like any other group of people brought together by long hours of work time. Sometimes we bickered, complained, and got on each other's nerves. As cool as she was, Millicent still had to behave in the role of supervisor because she had her own supervisor to report to. Therefore, she had the not always pleasant task of reviewing job performances, as well as enforcing punctuality and attendance. No matter how cool or fun any boss is, that person is still the authority in a chain of command, but Millicent managed to strike a mostly likable balance among us.

This was my first *real* work-family. In the almost four years of working for CMT, the racial ratio seemed to always be the same: three Blacks to four whites. We discussed our racial differences more as a matter of curiosity more than political leanings, sharing food recipes from the cultures we represented—Black American, Caribbean, Latinx, Irish, and Italian. We swapped family stories, talked about shared values, and told funny stories about our stumbles into adulthood.

Prior to this full-on adult lifestyle, my friendships were usually held together by the glue of alcohol via parties and reunions with high school and college friends for special occasions like birthdays or holidays. Once I lost touch with the old friends (other than stray phone calls to catch each other up) and work- and home-life became priority, the co-workers became *my people* in a way I didn't anticipate. We spent time in each other's homes, celebrating holidays together, having barbecues, and cooking weekend dinners.

While I'd gotten a taste of this kind of socializing as a young adult in college, it didn't have the same feeling of permanency. We were cooking in our dorms and in temporary off-campus dwellings. We fully expected those kinds of get-togethers to end when our college days ended. Permanent jobs drew us away from each other into differing cities.

My life as an employee with the CMT exposed me to an entirely new way of being. With rare exceptions, most of my childhood was spent with a family who kept to themselves. Occasionally, because I'd spent most of childhood being best friends with the same girl from a family living in close proximity to my home, I was sometimes allowed to spend special celebrations with them. But more often, due to my father's domineering control over our household, our family lived an insular kind of existence. There were no barbecues with neighbors. There were no family reunions or picnics. There were no dinner parties where invitees showed up with a dish of food or a bottle of wine. I experienced none of that! I knew it existed, read about get-togethers in books, and saw television families experiencing it. However, the consorting and fraternizing lifestyle of adults in community was as familiar to me as building airplanes or journeying on an African safari. It didn't happen.

This new life among working people was a healing balm for my heart and soul. To my surprise, most of the key players—the ones who helped me to find my footing as a working professional, as a new mother, as a wife and as a healthy adjusting adult—were white people. In those days, while I kept my past hidden and battled privately with depression, I was also awash with the love and generosity of people like Millicent and the CMT co-workers.

What about the Black co-workers, one might wonder? Weren't they enough? Why did I seem to gravitate towards the white co-workers instead of the Black co-workers? The short answer is, just because there are a number of Black people in one environment doesn't mean they have enough in common to be friends with each other. Blackness doesn't make us identical. We come from an array of experiences just like any other group. While the Blacks I worked with back then were awesome and beautiful too, we didn't have a lot in common. Sometimes they were men, sometimes they were older than me, and sometimes they were young, single people without children. In retrospect, I was also probably more needy and open to new relationships than my Black co-workers were. As a result, I spent more time with those who were open too. It just so happened they were white people.

Writer/Comedian Amanda Seales is known to describe white people in two distinct categories. According to Amanda, there are *white people* and then there are people who just *happen to be white*. Members of the latter group are the ones some Black people enjoy close relationships with. People who *happen to be white* are allies to people of color; they're loyal and reliable in their friendships with others not of their race. Their whiteness is incidental. They're unafraid of racial conversations and they don't live in constant apology about racism. People who *happen to be white* work to be an active part in the solution for equal treatment of all people, regardless of skin color. Amanda's general description of *white people*, on the other hand is, these are the ones who prefer to maintain the status quo—living in their white supremacist given privilege, benefitting from gains afforded them by unfair laws which keep the underclass and under-privileged in lesser positions of opportunity.

The angels who landed on my path in the 1990s just *happened to be white*.

There is one angel in particular from that season of my life who showed up and changed everything.

The CMT had a vacancy to fill when Millicent got married and moved to another state after working with us for a year. Between recommendations from Millicent and the managing supervisor from the umbrella agency which employed me—their referrals were extremely favorable and enthusiastic; having no MSW degree, I would never have gotten the supervisor job without those two women, who just happen to be white—I was promoted to the supervisor position at the CMT. Shortly after my promotion, due to increased funding, the agency was able to hire its first administrative assistant, an Irish woman who was at once disarmingly maternal to us and became a sort of wise mentor in the office.

Kathleen (not her real name) was about eight years older than me, a divorced mother of two, and a real wise-ass. Whereas Millicent had introduced me to hippy-love mixed with corporate-like professionalism, Kathleen introduced me to a mother-earthly feminism and a streetwise demeanor that I'd previously thought was unheard of among white women. Before meeting Kathleen, I thought most white women were soft-spoken, demure, and genteel (all descriptions, by the way, which made a rebellious city girl like me roll her eyes). Imagine my relief—not right away, of course; I was still adjusting to my new role as supervisor—when Kathleen surprised me in a public display of shenanigans meant to embarrass and soothe me simultaneously.

Since career life was still new to me, outside lunch trips with co-workers were relatively unfamiliar. Decades of office working life would eventually lead to routine lunches with colleagues and business associates. But back in the 1990s, this was all still new to me.

Kathleen and I had spent weeks sorting through files that were years old and needed archiving. She was extremely organized and also, no-nonsense and practical about suggestions for revamping our filing system to improve workflow. During the filing and refiling, we exchanged stories about motherhood and family life. Kathleen talked more than I did because she was clearly more comfortable in her skin and more open about her life than I was. But also, she was *funny*. All this time, after using humor and clownish behavior at home, I thought *I* was so funny. Kathleen was hilarious! Whereas I used my humor to deflect and protect, Kathleen was just being herself, someone comfortable in her own skin.

We usually brought our lunches from home. Or someone in the office would make a fast-food run after taking orders. On this particular day, everyone was out in the field. Kathleen and I were the only ones in the office. She suggested we go to Burger King for lunch.

I wasn't yet self-aware and it was too early in adulthood for me to know the difference between the bravado I tended to display as a show of confidence. (I explained the distinction between these two traits two chapters ago).

As a defense, I'd already begun building walls around my heart. I was desperate to maintain my own safety, to control my environment as much as possible. Sometimes I went overboard with trying to control things around me.

The two of us were standing in line in Burger King and it was our turn to order. We step up to the counter and for one unintentional moment, I let my work-mask slip because fast-food restaurants were usually from my weekend life. We're in Upstate New York and the Burger Kings there make the sandwiches differently than the Burger Kings I'm used to in Brooklyn. This was a point of extreme irritation for me back then.

(I want to say something clever here to defend my OCD disdain for the Burger Kings of Upstate New York from those days. But I've got nothing).

While ordering, I start giving explicit directions on how to make my burger. I have no idea Kathleen is studying me with amusement. I end my order with a veiled warning: *make sure you tell them I do* not *want ANY MUSTARD on my burger*.

At this point Kathleen drapes an arm around my shoulder, ignoring my surprise at the sudden intimacy and addresses the hapless Burger King cashier. In my mind, I'm flipping out: why is this woman touching me? Because the other thing is, I think I'm tough because I'm a Black girl from Brooklyn. I also think I'm tough because I came from a violent home. Kathleen is white and I'm looking at her like she's lost her mind. Based on my accumulated knowledge up to that point—as in, based on my tv show viewings—all white women are docile, reserved, and demure. And they don't go around hugging Black people they barely know. *How dare she!* I remember thinking, *How dare this crazy white woman touch me like I'm her child!* I wanted to claw her face.

But it was what Kathleen said to the cashier that stunned me, the words that gave me pause, mere milliseconds to choose my next move carefully. Leaning in with an intentional stage whisper, Kathleen says, *Oh yes, please! You do NOT want to go putting mustard on that burger because mustard interferes with her medication.* She gave a slight nod, never taking her eyes off the cashier until that cashier nodded back.

My jaw dropped. For a second, I couldn't speak. I stared at Kathleen's profile, trying to decide what to say or do, until she finally turned—her arm still firmly around my shoulders—and looked at me, raising her eyebrows like a dare. When our eyes met and I saw the way they danced with mischief, we both burst into relieved laughter. Because she *knew* she had me. What could I do in response without looking like an actual lunatic? I had to play along. And the truth is, it was funny!

Kathleen proved to be one of the best friends I never knew I needed.

I don't know what life might have been like if I'd entered motherhood around Black people, around Black friends. But I didn't. When I first became a mother, I was learning motherhood surrounded mainly by white friends. And those friends stepped up in the most unexpected and generous ways.

Kathleen never looked at me as if to say, this is how it's done. She just lived her single-parent life proudly and with a big heart that was opened to me. We spent time in each other's apartments. We babysat for each other. I watched the way Kathleen interacted with her own two young daughters and I learned about loving children without condition, allowing them room to grow and be themselves. Honestly? As I watched Kathleen in her role as a mother, I had to remind myself not to gawk. She was beyond patient with her toddler, even when that child was demanding or tired with crankiness.

When I look back on that period, I know Kathleen was an angel, someone who opened her heart because it was just who she was, a woman who stayed friendly with an ex-husband for the sake of the children she adored. When my own first marriage ended during that same season, it was Kathleen and her ex-husband who showed up to help me move into a smaller, more affordable apartment.

Sadly, we drifted apart as we made different moves for our lives. Kathleen moved to a neighboring city to buy her first house. A few years later, I left the cold and often dreary weather of Upstate New York to build a new life in sunny Florida. Initially, we both committed to keeping in touch, routinely calling and sending letters (oh how I miss the letter-writing days between friends!) until life changes—new priorities, time passing, and the long-distance—finally pushed us further apart.

I've heard it said that some friendships are meant to last for limited seasons. However, what I would add is, that doesn't mean they become less important or less impactful in the lives of the people they touch. My CMT work-family entered life for me at exactly the right time. I was a young wife and mother in her formative adult years. The relationships which bloomed during that era provided a soft place for me to land in The World, even if only for a handful of years.

Angels.

They've always shown up exactly when I needed them the most.

18

THE *BLACK IS KING* FILM – AM I A CULTURAL CRITIC?

Remember back in chapter fifteen, where I talked about writers being taken by surprise by detours of an unfolding story? And remember even further back, when in chapter four I talked about how this book was supposed to be all blog essays? Well, it's happening again. This chapter has taken a sharp directional turn and I am following it.

As I stopped and noted the main ideas of each chapter, it occurred to me that maybe I should explain the pause I was experiencing. Maybe I should write this chapter differently. So that's what's happening. The majority of this book is about a period of real-time events. I'm basically capturing six months of my writing life with some flashback stories woven in. I've written about writing episodes as they unfolded—editing blog essays, being mortified by the blog content, hitting the delete button in excess, panicking, freaking out, writing all-new essays from scratch.

When I first wrote this chapter, it was all about my reaction to Beyoncé's *Black Is King* film. I wrote it—in August 2020—three days after seeing Beyoncé's hour-long musical production. Two months later, by the time I got to the third draft of this book, I asked myself some questions. What's this chapter really about? Are you a cultural critic now? What about all the commentary you shared in the earlier chapters about your own mental health and behavioral development? Are you a psychologist? Are you a scientist? An anthropologist? A political commentator? Do you have *any* credentials giving you the authority to discuss the contents in this book?

No, I don't. Not if we're talking about paper credentials issued by boards and schools.

However, I have something else.

What I *do* have is the body I exist in as a live human being on the planet. I really don't need permission to talk about my own body.

What I *do* have is my experience as an adult Black woman in the world. Any woman who's ever been a daughter can offer her wise insight into her own daughterly experiences. Any woman who's been a mother can offer insight based on her lessons learned as a mother. And anyone who's gone through any number of years being Black can talk about Blackness.

What I *do* have is the freedom given me by birthright to be and do whatever I want, the same as everyone else. All these things are my credentials.

Additionally, our times have changed. Ordinary, everyday people are beginning to stand up more often to lend their voice. We're telling our own stories, adding our perspective as a version of the human experience, letting the world know that we were here too, and this is what we felt and saw. Some of us are using YouTube or our blogs or Instagram or whatever social media we frequent as a platform to be seen and heard. Some of us are in community—meeting together formally or socially, online, in our homes, in churches, in community centers, in gyms, at parks, and wherever else it's convenient for two or more to gather and share ideas.

This is our time. We're in the midst of a seismic evolutionary shift in history. Similar to this book in your hands, our human story is still unfolding, and the history of us—who we all are—is being recorded before the story actually ends. The fact is, there *is* no end until we're all gone, until there's no more human life left on the planet. This is our time because we're no longer beholden to the more powerful, wealthier, and more connected among us to be the record keepers of the Human Story.

I can't lie and say this is easy because it's not. The reality is, this is awkward as fuck. It's awkward because there aren't enough examples of reverse hierarchy kinds of books which are elevated and accessible to us all, books where behavioral development is explained from the trenches of the human experience. Yes, there are memoirs where writers share their personal stories while also offering commentary on history and culture, but they aren't plentiful enough for me to say I've found precedents—and therefore have book examples to draw on—which are relatable to my own personal experience. And also, those writers tend to be more credentialed than the average person. I don't have enough schooling or field experience to be deemed, by hierarchal authority, a reliable expert on these topics.

Based on what I was taught, we're supposed to trust the experts and trust the books that those experts write. I did that, trusted the experts in the world for a long time, well into adulthood. When, as a child, I was sent to public school, there was a collective expectation—among the government, my teachers, my parents, and even me as a kid—that I would be taught all the things I needed to know to become successful in whichever career or vocation I eventually chose. Also, based on what I learned, if I enjoyed reading and wanted to continue diving into books, I was free to continue my learning with access to even more books on wider topics and genres, in bookstores, in libraries, and online.

On one hand, I was not disappointed. Public school did its job and I went on to find employment with livelihoods which helped me meet my own needs and take care of a family. Additionally, in my downtime, I could read all kinds of books to satisfy my personal tastes—there were books galore in brick and mortar stores, online, and in libraries. All good, right? Wrong. Because on the other hand, as a Black person, my history was deliberately altered, and large chunks omitted from the books I was learning from in the schools. Also, on the other hand, when it came to leisurely reading, there weren't a lot of books written by Black people. Oh yeah, sure we've made some strides.

The literary world has finally—after being pressed for centuries by Black scholars who found inventive ways to be heard and have their books published—unveiled a treasure trove of books by talented Black writers. But we still have a long way to go on that note. I mean, a really *really* long way to go. Because the truth is, while the number of high school and college graduates among Blacks has grown exponentially since the 1960s, illiteracy rates among us have also increased. According to the 2015 National Assessment of Educational Progress, fourth-grade African-American students lag behind white students in reading and math proficiency by as much as twenty percent.

The other awkward part of writing all this for me is, based on the design of our social structure, as an ordinary person without credentials, it's not my place to be writing about my own plight. But I'm writing about these things regardless because Black people—*my people*—are still struggling and falling behind academically. Black people are intelligent and talented—not just in sports and entertainment—in a million different ways. The fact that so many of us come across as uninterested in reading is not an accurate measurement of our intelligence. The disinterest by so many Black people in reading books is more a reflection of the types of books that have been historically available to us to read. Textbooks and other non-fiction books continue to be primarily authored by whites who are biased in their depiction of the Human Story. The spectrum of available fiction books has broadened with diversity, but not enough to whet the reading appetites of *all* people of color. Thanks to progress, the non-fiction and fiction book selections have benefitted from the influx of talented writers increasingly from previously underrepresented and discriminated against groups of all colors, sexual orientations, and ethnicities. However, we still need more. We're still playing catch up towards equal footing in the patriarchy.

But who am I to be saying these things? Especially if this is supposed to be a memoir. Well, as uncomfortable as it feels to find the words to say all these things—like I said, awkward—I'm saying it because we can't change what we can't (or won't) see. I'm saying it because, while there may already be proper scientists and social critics putting their research about us—Black people—into books, those books are not helping us to improve because a lot of us are never going to read those studies. The hierarchal social design is too rigid and discriminating to be relied upon as a method for advancing the interest and progress of Black people. On behalf of those of us—in the human trenches, ordinary working folk—who are Black cogs in the wheel of social order, I'm putting in my two cents of thoughts on these matters.

As for the less readerly-inclined among us? I'm not really sure what the answers are. However, based on our shared past, based on the Black women I met during my research, and based on my own personal circle of loved ones, I know what the answers are NOT. Most of the textbooks being used in public schools to teach our children are terrible and should be tossed into the trash. Additionally, we need more books by Black authors on bookshelves and online. I'm not saying everyone needs to start writing books. Writing is not always as fun as it looks. It's hard work! But for the Black people reading, I know you understand that in addition to all our other struggles, this issue is yet another one that we really need to look at. Every single one of us has something unique and wise to contribute when it comes to potential solutions to assist in the support and progress of Black people. At least if we're talking about it (more often than we already are), making it such a frequently visited topic, we can inspire increased interest in reading and writing among the younger generation. But first, we might want to consider some truths about how *not* discussing this (more often) might be contributing to the existing problems of our literacy deficits.

For instance, here's a little more truth on the matter. While I do appreciate the whole movement some of us are about in the field of *Black excellence*, there are large numbers of us who might feel excluded from the concept of *Black excellence* and are getting left behind as a result. I have a college degree, but having a college degree doesn't make me smarter or better than someone without a college degree. It makes me fortunate and it makes me privileged, especially in light of the overwhelming number of Black people who didn't have the luxury of time or opportunity to go to college because getting a job in order to pay bills—to keep their family surviving, to keep their heads above water—was the most important priority. I'm sure I'm not the only person with a college degree who feels this way, who recognizes their privilege, and desires to bring others into the fold. We're all out here, with and without college degrees, trying to connect and help each other.

I may have graduated from college, but the people I've spent the majority of my life with and love dearly did not. They are just as wise and talented—often way more talented than they even realize because when you're busy surviving, so tied up in working for your own survival, you can forget how brilliant you actually are. I know how this feels—as anyone else. But how do we bridge the gaps between all of us? How do we give ourselves a reset on Black progress, reengaging with those of us who stopped seeing themselves in the larger picture of the Human Story? Like I said, I don't really know what all the answers are. What I know is what it's like to feel left out. And I also know that not every Black youth and Black adult feels included in the concept and movement of celebrating *Black excellence*.

If I close my eyes right now and can see the face of even one Black child or adult that I know personally who would have no idea what I was talking about if I referenced the term, *Black excellence*, then I know that every Black person reading this can think of someone too. This means, there are large enough numbers of us feeling excluded for us to be concerned about a progressive Black movement, which leaves increasing numbers of other Blacks behind. I know it's hard to include everyone—especially if disinterest is the presenting obvious factor—but I don't think we can expect to keep moving forward if we continue to lean on that excuse. It's going to catch up and hurt us in the long run.

I'm just a woman willing to endure a little discomfort by starting an awkward conversation. I guess it's because of my background. I've spent so many of my years feeling on the outside of nearly everything, that it began to serve me as a writer/researcher.

Do you remember your childhood? Do you remember being in the classroom or the lunchroom and noticing the extremely quiet kids among all the noisy kids? Maybe *you* were actually one of the quiet kids. Of course, now that I'm older, I know that kids can be quiet for any number of reasons, including boredom or homesickness or self-esteem issues. I remember those days sometimes like it was yesterday. Being in school with all those hundreds of clamoring, noisy bodies, trying to fit in, and trying to find your own little tribe of spirit-animals.

When I look back on that time, all those decades ago, I can see now that most of the time, I ended up in friendships where the friends chose me, and not the other way around, because I was one of the quiet ones. As previously stated, I'd always been insecure and uncomfortable in my own skin. But it wasn't all bad because it made me a people-watcher. I was so often perplexed by human dynamics that I made it my mission to understand as much as I could about our behaviors and about what drove each of us to do the things we do.

It's the quiet ones among us who tend to feel excluded, get more quiet with age, and eventually get left behind as society progresses.

In recent years, I've read a lot of excellent books by Black authors—the credentialed, celebrated thinkers and cultural critics among us—who've written about our race and how racism impacted us historically. Writers like bell hooks, Audre Lorde, and Alice Walker, for example. Based on my cumulative reading knowledge coupled with my own personal observations, I've come to realize, as Black people, we often reveal conflicting outlooks on our views of Black celebrities.

I'll use myself, for example. In chapter fifteen, when I first talked about Beyoncé's *Homecoming* concert, I admitted to being jealous of her and her dancers. I didn't mind admitting that because now that I'm older, I understand how natural it is for us as humans to sometimes be jealous of each other. Jealousy falls on the spectrum of emotions that we all experience. But for some reason, it's a taboo topic that we don't ordinarily talk about unless we're shaming someone for displaying their jealousy. We call them *haters* and we discuss them freely in our social world as if the haters have an affliction that we know very little about.

For Black people, I think our jealousy is made more complicated because of the racist oppression we live under in American culture. While we don't feel discriminated against or racially tyrannized in every moment, we do always exist under the cloud of a generally racist culture that impacts our outlook. So when I see Beyoncé winning at life, making a lot of money, having fame, and appearing to be living her best life, I'm thinking about the unfairness of it all. I'm looking at a Black woman—Beyoncé—who appears to be less impacted by the cloud of racism we're all trapped under than I am. And I think, *No fair!*

On one hand, I'm proud to be connected to Beyoncé's success by virtue of my Blackness. When The World looks at me or any other Black woman, maybe we're viewed with higher regard thanks to the visibility of a celebrity like Beyoncé. But on the other hand, I'll sometimes experience feelings of jealousy about Beyoncé's success, which makes it harder to root for her or even like her. I'm sure I'm not the only Black person who has felt this way about a Black celebrity, but it's a sore spot which we're not really talking too much about (or talking at all about).

It's not just Beyoncé, it's *all* the wealthy Black celebrities our community has tended to love and hate simultaneously and incongruously as Black people. Oprah, Kanye, Denzel, Alicia Keys, Serena Williams, Gabrielle Union, Tyra, Jada, Viola, and many more. As normal as it should be to feel this way—hating or disliking them because they have more than we have— to me, it also feels uncomfortable. Because we live in such an oppressive society, we need each other's support to progress. We really don't have the luxury of turning our backs on each other in such perilous times as these. When it comes to oppression—no matter how wealthy, disenfranchised, or middle of the road our finances are—*none* of us are free until *all* of us are free. That goes for sexual orientation, gender identities, skin color, and ethnic background.

Even though I've experienced mixed feelings about Beyoncé in the past, the truth is I respect her and admire her tremendously. In my home, where we've— especially my daughters and I—discussed Beyoncé's musical creations with excitement, she's considered a queen. And yet, *Black Is King* brought my respect and admiration for her to an even higher level. As a woman who was once the quiet kid, the kid who was quiet because she thought herself unworthy, the *Black Is King* message landed squarely on my heart with resounding resonance.

I was already excited about the kind of message *Black Is King* might bring because of Beyoncé's *Lemonade* album and because of *Homecoming*. To me, *Lemonade* was exactly the kind of memoir/social-commentary/from-the-trenches-of-human-pain type of artistry I'd been searching for to give me courage as a storyteller and as an eventual memoirist. I know how hard that is, to take all your hurts and all your disappointments about life and turn it into an artistic product for public consumption. It feels extremely vulnerable and scary, but you do it anyway because, quite possibly, you've drawn inspiration from an artist who produced their own version of transformed heartbreak.

After all the hype—all the promos I'd seen on YouTube and other social media—Beyoncé's *Black Is King* film did ***not*** disappoint. This spectacular collage of music videos made me feel incredibly SEEN as one of the quiet kids, the kid who thought she was unwanted and wrong all over, especially in her physical appearance. *Black Is King* provided an hour of enjoyable music through which I could see myself differently.

I saw *me* in all my parts. I saw my skin color, au latte brown. I saw my hair, dreadlocked and shaved. I saw my nose, African in shape. I saw my lips, darkened with age. I saw my brown eyes. I saw my come hither, swinging hips and my fat, round butt. I saw my occasional sneer and attitude. I saw my rowdy laugh. I saw my genius. I saw my juicy thighs and spread legs. I saw my proud, defiantly gawking eyes. I saw my arrested shame, no longer hovering over me. I saw my vulnerability. I saw my fear. I saw my big, hopeful heart. I saw my sexuality. I saw my power. I saw my desire. I saw my tears. I saw my goofy, wide smile.

Because, where have I been all these years in American stories—television shows, movies, music, and all other media—besides being completely invisible or partially represented or white-washed? I've spent my whole life overreaching, acting as if a television character represented me—in appearance, in language, in attitude or in perspectives—if I squint really hard and use my imagination. TV never got it right.

Yes, I can agree that television depictions of Black people have made significant improvements, becoming better at moving beyond previous caricatures and stereotypes (not completely, but still, some progress has been made). However, I continue to view character portrayals that are fractionally representative of the kind of woman I am.

Along comes *Black Is King* and—finally! —there I am, live and in living color, in the bodies of a plethora of beautiful Black people, women and men alike.

I even saw Caribbeans in Beyoncé's film musical! Not just Caribbeans but Caribbeans with REAL accents. Musical sounds of reggae from my own Jamaican family history actually shared the same airtime as African and African-American vibes, as well as vibes of multiple shades of additional brown-skinned cultures. All the gorgeous shades of Blackness in one place! Who'da thunk it possible? We've been so accustomed to the idea of America being some kind of "melting pot" or "salad bowl" or some other supposed mix of included ingredients.

All my life, I'd been searching and wondering, who—meaning, the collective who. Not just one person; what movement or which group—was going to step forward to help those of us who felt left behind and forgotten by society. Despite a rough start, I tried to keep going in the world, did my best to build a life. I worked, I raised kids, I married, I paid bills, I partook in most of America's socially trending traditions.

But I ached and I hurt. I spent a lot of time in my wounds. My heart was broken, even as I smiled and spread what I could of the love I was fortunate enough to sometimes feel.

Because the truth is, I was a lost girl for a really long time.

People of color have been routinely—and deliberately—left out of the American story. And whenever we were written in, the narrative was arranged to suit white people, to make white people look ever powerful and superior. And I used to think, well shit, at least I'm not alone. I have American classism, racism and varieties of discrimination to comfort me on days when I'm feeling alone, unloved and unseen because large numbers of other people are also left out. Mainly, I thought American racism gave me a default, oversized family to belong to.

And yet, what became increasingly clear as I grew older was, Black people didn't see me either.

The other truth was, I often felt completely on the outside of all things Blackness.

I simply didn't belong anywhere or to any particular group that I could see. Because at the end of the day, we must each return to the homes we live in. It doesn't matter how many friends you have or how often you get together with people or how much time you and your homies spend on the phone gossiping and sharing stories. Those moments are mere slices of life. The social world and the people in it are merely extensions of our central lives. Real-life begins with the nuclear family, starting with the caregivers assigned to us as children.

Since the beginning of time, our central lives have begun with The Family we're born into. After fifty-four years of life on the planet, I learned that without belonging—feeling unrooted by the disconnect from one's parents—solitary feelings can force you into society's margins.

In young adulthood, I didn't think my broken family life would be a big deal. All I cared about back then was being free to go forward to create my own life. All I cared about was being safe, finally. In my new life of independence, I was thrilled at the prospect of possessing myself, owning my mind, and especially owning my body for the first time. I would suffer no more rapes by my father and be shielded from the open bitterness and hostility of my mother. There would be no more violence, no more beatings at their hands.

My childhood lay behind me like strewn, outgrown clothes and toys. New adulthood stood before me like a glowing beacon of life-giving light. I thought the future looked golden.

And it was …. sometimes.

I made a sweet life for myself, even if there were some bitter stretches of days. Like the rest of the humans, my life unfolded into peaks and valleys—I learned to take the bad days with the good days. I learned to make the best of life's difficulties. I got better at multiplying splendid days and managed to create a life with wonderful memories. I had beautiful children. In the second marriage, I married an amazing man, more nurturing and more loving than anyone I'd ever known.

But whenever things were quiet and I was alone, I privately struggled. Every once in a while—after a stretch of good days, weeks, or months—something would happen, a trigger, reminding me of the part of my heart that randomly felt sad and broken. Feelings of longing would emerge. As a result of breaking the ties with my childhood family because they were simply too toxic—staying connected would have compromised my own mental health. There was a generally bitter outlook on life shared by my parents and siblings; to stay connected meant frequent fighting with them on too many levels—I felt like a perpetual outsider to the rest of the world.

I thought my Blackness, making connections with other Blacks in The World, would be the thing to eventually save me. I thought that since people of color were so pervasively discriminated against, there'd be enough numbers of us to draw together for support. And I'm not saying we haven't tried. We have. There've been compassionate and excellent movements on behalf of Black people across the generations. Additionally, on smaller scales, there've been community groups and (nowadays, we have) online social platforms.

But these kinds of groups were hard to find. Making community connections wasn't as simple as I thought it would be. I've often felt like someone who went to the party or to the barbecue or to the block party or to the parade and ended up returning to her home, only to feel more alone than she felt before she spent time in the company of all the revelers. Because while we were all together, even though most of us were laughing and smiling, it still felt like I had to keep my guards up. Sometimes I felt insecure. Sometimes I felt judging eyes on my clothes and on my body. Sometimes I felt like I was saying the wrong things. Sometimes I felt out of place. Sometimes I wanted to cry because I couldn't tell what was real and genuine from what felt fake and pretentious. Sometimes I wondered what it might be like if I expressed what I was feeling in the moment, at the gatherings. I wondered if anyone felt it too.

More than anything, I felt like I didn't matter.

Beyoncé doesn't know me, has never met me, and has never spoken to me directly. And yet, in the words of her songs and in her film, *Black Is King*, she lets me know that she SEES me. She lets me know that she is very aware of my outsider feelings and the almost agonizing and hungry ways I've wanted to belong as a Black girl in the world. The message delivered—loud and clear—by Beyoncé's film is, my belonging existed before I was even born. My belonging is not stipulated on being a part of a loving family or being active in a community that knows who I am or trying to fit into behaviors foreign and/or unnatural to me.

For so many years, I felt like an oddball watching entertainment and reading books that spoke so frequently of loving family ties. How could I not feel a kind of ostracization reading about mothers and fathers being heroes to writers of books which heralded their family messages? Yes, I love my own family, the children I have and the husband I'm partnered with. But the history of who I am is still alive. I'm still the little girl I used to be, even if I'm all grown up now. I straddle two worlds, belonging to two differing family experiences, past and present. The experience of both made me who I am.

Beyoncé found a way—departing from the rigidity of patriarchal diversity—to embrace ALL Black and brown people without making us feel like we have to squint our eyes and use our imaginations to find little more than slices of ourselves in her presentations. The message delivered—loud and clear! —by the film is, every single Black person is a king or queen.

The message came as a reminder to me that it's never too late. It's never too late to become your more amazing self. It's never too late to embrace a new message. It's never too late to find a book or find a song or find a movement that actually sees you, inspiring you with new hope.

I rewrote this chapter to say that it isn't all about Beyoncé. This is about us. It's about what's possible if we allow the harder truths about all our lives to surface more.

19

HAPPILY MARRIED AND THE MESSES
IN BETWEEN

I saved this chapter to write last even though it doesn't appear last in the book. I thought writing this chapter was going to be a cakewalk because it was supposed to be about how I eventually found my own true love and how proud I learned to be about my love life instead of continuing to shrink like it was something to be ashamed of.

After struggling for weeks to write this, I finally stopped this afternoon and took a walk. It was a chilly and cloudy October day. I had earbuds plugged into a favored playlist. When two minutes into the walk an India Arie song brought a puddle of tears, I simply let them roll from behind the dark sunglasses and wet my already cold cheeks. I've no idea if the drivers in the three cars which drifted slowly by could see that I was crying.

As I tilted my head back, staring into pockets of vague sunlight behind drifting gray clouds, I was searching for answers because—why was this particular chapter giving me a hard time? *Just write the truth for fuck's sake.*

Fine.

Thirty-five minutes later, back inside my cold living room—because I refuse to turn the heat on so early in October—I started re-writing this chapter.

I was going to intellectualize about landing in a happy second marriage after surviving an abusive childhood. I was going to talk about Black men in America, share thoughts about my father, lament on the importance of forgiveness, and then tie it all together. I wrote those things, but it all sounded wrong, like they were coming from a stranger. It sounded disconnected, like I was trying to give a clinical report on my own love life.

On the walk earlier this afternoon, five-year-old me showed up. I saw my face when I was still a newcomer in America, during a time when everything once familiar—the island where I was born, the home I'd grown up in, all the cousins and friends I used to play with—was suddenly gone for good, without ceremony or explanation. For months my eyes were wide with shock and grief. I'd left behind a grandmother who I adored, the only adult—before I met Howard—who'd ever made me feel unconditionally safe and loved. I'd stopped thinking about that time and what it was like for me, how terribly confused and sad I was for so long. There hadn't been time for grief over my vanished Jamaican life because I now had a new environment to survive, new caregivers to adjust to. That was almost fifty years ago.

I'm amazed at how easy it is to give up and stop hoping, expecting it all to get worse. I did that for a while, back when I was still drinking. I slipped into dead-eyes and lived on autopilot, did only as much as I needed to do to get by. I marvel now at the way my body's instinct for survival kicked on, forced me to wake up and fight for a better way of life, fight to do more than just survive. I don't know how I could have known to hope, how I knew that I shouldn't give up.

I was thirty-seven when I met Howard. He was moonlighting in Home Depot, working behind the counter in the paint department, when I was walking by. Howard Archer found me when the hope inside me was a mere glimmer of flickering light, despite my eleven years as a divorced, single-parent. On that day in Home Depot, Howard was so sincerely excited to remember me as the same girl he knew in middle school, he flashed the kind of unassuming smile that I knew was real. I didn't remember him, but I knew he was telling the truth and it wasn't a pick-up line.

After seventeen years of marriage, I still have a crush on Howard. I still can't believe my good fortune, that my life transformed and became amazing. As women in the patriarchy, there are so many demands placed upon us from all levels and groups of people, so many ways we're expected to behave, numerous restrictions and expectations. Howard was the first person to meet me exactly where I was and who allowed me to be my entire flawed self. Such a relief! I didn't know how exhausted I'd been with all the ways I'd contorted to fit images not my own until I met him.

We'd each been disappointed by life. We'd each had our hearts broken. We were both terribly flawed. We'd both been hapless and clueless. *What?* Yes. I think this was our favorite part about each other. We'd each been the suckers in the sucker-games of life. It made us fast friends who became the best of friends.

Why was it so hard to write these things? Because there is still a part of me that I tussle with, the part which sees herself as unworthy and undeserving of good fortune. How dare I flaunt my happiness? Especially in these difficult and uncertain times? Who do I think I am?

Here's the thing I'm thinking though. Why feed hopeless sentiments? Why shouldn't we shine a little of our light during the dark times? What's the point in collectively feeling gloomy, bitter, or hopeless?

Who do I think I am? I think I'm not much different than anyone reading these words. I still hurt. My life is messy, even as I write this. I want to stand and be seen in the messiness, step into it more deeply, the way you step into muddy waters after a flood, as you salvage what remains. I want to also shine, reminding The World about its own beauty, about the fact that in the midst of heartbreak and sadness, there is still love.

The pain of early beginnings had to have been leading me somewhere. Our lives of suffering intersect to teach us, I think.

Last weekend, Howard and I went out to eat and sat down for lunch inside of a restaurant—Texas Roadhouse—for the first time since the quarantine began seven months ago. We were so jubilant we couldn't stop smiling and whispering exclamations to each other about our good fortune. It was so long since we'd eaten inside of a restaurant. It was beginning to feel like dining out was never going to happen again. We ordered all of our favorite selections, knowing we'd never be able to finish all that food. Of course, we ended up taking our leftovers home.

What I can tell you about marriage the second time around is, if I've learned nothing else, it taught me to keep believing in hope. I met my goateed, handsome hubby when I least expected to meet someone, when I wasn't even looking to meet anyone. Here was a Black man who was seemingly undaunted by an often unfair world, who after his own failed first marriage, had kept his heart open and held on to the hope that he would eventually find a truer love for himself.

The morning after our lunch at Texas Roadhouse— Sunday—Howard and I did the same thing we do every weekend. We goofed off like a couple of teenagers, drinking coffee in bed, and chatting about our separate work weeks. During long, comfortable silences, I'd lean on him, laying my head on his shoulder and be pleasantly surprised by his kiss on my forehead. I still get butterflies whenever he does this because it's just one more reminder that I am indeed safe and I am indeed loved.

I tell Howard all the time, he's the most beautiful person among men and women that I've ever met. In the seventeen years we've been married, he's never felt a need to tone down his expressions of love for me. We're hand-holders in public. We lock eyes in crowded rooms.

We cheer each other's small victories. We flirt, give pats or squeezes on our butts, we giggle, and we wink at one another. In a world that often feels like there's an overwhelming sentiment against marriage, we enjoy cherishing the gift of our own matrimony. It's one more way of us agreeing to never give up, one more way to avoid cynicism.

I'm so over trying to appear as only one thing at a time, as merely one thing or the other. I'm all the things that a nuanced life inspires. Life may have brought difficulties, but I'm not perpetually broken. And yet, just because I overcame obstacles doesn't mean that hurt and occasional sadness are a thing of the permanent past.

But also, I fell in love with someone extraordinary and we're living the dreamy happily ever after love story. This is how it looks to stand up in the dissonant and conflicting experiences of life—feeling giddy in love one minute, then confused by life's overwhelm, only to move into sad memories of heartbreaks, all while remaining hopeful enough to stop shrinking and shine a light anyway.

The past keeps informing the present and the future—who I was, who I am, and who I'm still trying to be.

20

CONNECTING THE DOTS

It shouldn't have been such a big deal to chase this dream.

Writing is the one thing I've been passionate about since I was five. When I write, I come alive more as a person during the actual writing process than as the person doing something else. Writing breathes a kind of life into me like nothing else. When I'm writing, I'm like a fish sluicing through her watery habitat. All I need is a blank page and something to write with and I'm home, no matter where I am—in a hotel room, in a waiting room, on a plane, in a park, in line at a bank, in a taxi, or any other place in this world.

When I got the opportunity to quit the office job and spend entire days writing, it shouldn't have been as hard as it was. I'm not saying writing is easy because it isn't. But every person reading this—especially writers—who knows what it feels like to go to a job that they hate, how it feels to spend long hours in an environment which makes you feel like you're dying, also knows exactly what I'm talking about. There are thousands of artists in day jobs who would *love* to have the freedom to live life on their own terms—work from home, set their own hours, come and go as they please.

Once Howard and I looked at our finances and realized we could live on one salary, I should have been able to write happily ever after, even with the inevitable life bumps that everybody hits. I quit the job *four* years ago. That was over thirty-five THOUSAND HOURS ago. What the hell have I been doing? It's not like I was still working at the weekly forty-hour-work-week mill, stealing time to write whenever I could, bleary-eyed on a laptop at midnight or waking before the sun to write before leaving home to punch a clock elsewhere. I had the free hours that every employee dreams about with thoughts of hitting the lotto or finally reaching retirement bliss.

When a book idea found me and I figured out what was involved, once I developed surveys and questions for interviews, once I found, met, and talked with all the interested people, why couldn't I close the deal and produce a book?

I had to do things I didn't want to do first. I had to turn around and retrace my steps. Once I did that, retraced my steps, turned over every stone I could find blocking my path, documented all that I found— including reflective thoughts for this very essay—I was finally able to produce a manuscript that made sense. I'd been so frightened of all the unforeseen turns during the book writing process. But every time what seemed like a crazy inspiration found me and I did it, a revelation would follow to let me know it was the right thing to do.

While working on the first draft of this book, I stumbled on a Steve Jobs quote about *connecting the dots*. I found it in the pages of a book about the meteoric rise of Netflix during the wake of the fall of megacorporation, Blockbuster Video. The quote came from a commencement speech given by the billionaire business titan at the University of Stanford in 2005, six years before his death in 2011.

Nine years later, it's my turn to be impressed enough with this quote to include in my own book:

> *You can't connect the dots looking forward; you can only connect them looking backwards. So you have to trust that the dots will somehow connect in your future. You have to trust in something—your gut, destiny, life, karma, whatever. This approach has never let me down, and it has made all the difference in my life.*

When I first read that quote, my mouth dropped open. After rereading it a few times, I took a picture of it with my phone.

All throughout the writing of essays for this book, I'd wondered which quote I should use for the book's opening, as a way to introduce the content. I'd read so many books by different authors in my life, especially in the past four years—novelists, memoirists, rappers, scholars, scientists, songwriters, poets, filmmakers, etc. I have pages and pages of book quotes in journals and on my computer. Surely, if I was going to use a quote to capture the essence of my book—*surely!* —it would have to be a quote by a woman or a quote by a Black person. Right?

I stopped thinking about it because I knew my angels would reveal the answer exactly when I need it. I'd learned this along the writing journey, so I gave it no further thought, nearly forgetting about it entirely.

I knew almost immediately, as soon as the picture was taken, the Steve Jobs quote would be the one I'd use for the opening of this book.

But wait, what about the patriarchy? What about everything I wrote before about the oppressive, white male-centric social design, meant to advance the interest of white people while undermining the needs of women and people of color?

I know! I've been here with the angels—my gut, instinct, soul, heart, whatever—at least a dozen times, not trusting their directional cues immediately. I've resisted them, tried to disagree with them. But as I've learned in hard and soft ways, the angels are other-worldly, all-knowing souls, whereas I'm merely a flawed human with the tendency to over-rely primarily on what my eyes can see. I'd been in the habit of leaving over ninety percent of unused brain capacity to gather dust, living my life—according to well documented scientific research—using only the five percent brain capacity most of us tend to employ. At first, I was like, no fucking way. That can't be right. A white guy? After all my talk about racial tyranny, oppression, and misogyny? Do I really want to open my book with a quote by Steve Jobs? But I knew that was the right quote, whether I thought it made sense or not. White men are not the enemy. Hatred is our common enemy.

The patriarchy is a system, an infrastructure. The patriarchy is *not* individual people. Yes, the patriarchy is instituted and upheld by people, but the patriarchy isn't people. The patriarchy is a social construct. The patriarchy can be dismantled and replaced. Trust me. It's in the works. I don't have time to outline all the ways The World's brave and brilliant thinkers, change agents, and organizing giants are tirelessly working to make this happen. Google it. It's happening.

In the meantime, I had to admit, the quote encapsulated what I'd done by writing this book. As difficult as it was to do—because it began and ended with my pain and my tears so often—I connected the dots to get here. I asked myself the hard questions, I revisited painful seasons, and I told the truth as I saw it.

In routine conversations, when Howard and I review lessons learned from our respective workdays, I sometimes marvel that I can still wonder what life might have been like if I'd had a different kind of start. Maybe it's normal, something we all do as humans? Even though I do love the way my life turned out, love all the people in it, appreciate the wisdom I've gleaned from the seasons, my mind—in rare, small moments—will wander over to *what-if* territory, wondering what might have been. *What if I'd had loving parents and there was no abuse of any kind for me to overcome? What if there was never racism or I was born white? What if I believed in myself enough to go pursue a writing career sooner? What if I didn't wait until I was in my fifties to stop hating myself? What if I'd taken my life back sooner? What if I hadn't let Fear and Shame rule over me for so long?* As the thoughts spiraled, I'd play it off, offhandedly saying out loud to Howard, how it sure would have been nice to pursue writing sooner.

If I don't catch myself and pull back first, Howard will remind me to stop thinking that way because then we wouldn't be here, and maybe our kids wouldn't be here either, and maybe life wouldn't have turned out as well as it has so far. The grass on the other side is never as green as we think it is.

When I got stuck in the middle of writing the friendship book and realized I'd have to write a memoir first, I thought I was cursed. I felt cursed because the idea of abandoning the friendship book to write a memoir felt so scary in the beginning. I started ruing the day that I ever picked up pen and paper, ruing the day that I ever became enthralled with books, and ruing every single thing connected with writing. I didn't know (yet) that book writing could happen this way, that countless other writers before me had experienced this kind of book writing development. I learned to let go of only what my eyes could see, let go of what my limited perspective was showing me, and TRUST the process. I got into the habit of learning to rely more on instincts than on anything else.

I connected the dots.

I took a risk and stopped writing the friendship book. I didn't let fear stop me; instead, I allowed fear to ride shotgun with me. I've written some things in these pages that I never talked about with *anyone*, not even my own husband. I changed the way I thought about myself. I stopped being ashamed.

To the best of my ability to do so, I wiped my brain of its original programming, deleting as much as I could of the misinformation and propaganda fed to me throughout the decades, partially restoring to its previously blank settings. I'm a work in progress. I'll never wipe my entire brain slate clean, but neither will I give up trying to refresh.

I don't feel as intimidated as I used to by all the job titles, all the credentials, all the power, and all the billions of people with and without these things on the planet. When you really think about it—who are we other than a bunch of individuals sharing space on a planet? What is there to be ashamed of when we're all going through similar, opposing, and unique lives? We're all experiencing the emotions which come with our pain, our grief, our love, our happiness, and all the ups and downs. This is the way life goes. This is the paradox. This is our plight, each of us charged with the responsibility for figuring our circumstances out, making the necessary adjustments and contributions. Or not.

The alternative is becoming stagnant, choosing to stay stuck on whatever we think we already know. Like, for example, me thinking maybe I shouldn't preface my book with a Steve Jobs quote. But deciding to do so anyway. We can't allow ourselves to get stuck by letting difficulties and pain to hold us back or keep us from continuing to grow.

In no way am I minimizing the devastation of widespread deaths caused by a pandemic or murders due to racial tyranny. Nor am I negating the contributions and sacrifices made by individuals of *all* races who—in these scary and chaotic times— responded swiftly and bravely, confronting the crises with their voices, bodies, and their skills, demanding, seeking, and creating resolutions. Life inside the human family is complicated, creating complexities in the dynamics between us. It's hard as hell to *be* any of us— to live the life we're given—no matter how fabulous or dastardly we appear to each other. The individual choices we make from one moment to the next doesn't ever fully depict who any of us really are.

I used to tell my adult children that finding the elusive answer to the world's random display of ignorance and transgressions was our plight as Black people to deal with, that somehow it fell on each of us to know and do better. Like, oh well, it sucks to be us. Not so! Upon reflection inspired by writing these essays, I can now say I was wrong about that. That plight belongs to each and every one of us as human beings. The drudgery towards correcting humanity's course as we evolve, falls on every human shoulder— regardless of gender, skin color, class, sexual orientation, or nationality.

Yes, some of us *do* have more privilege than others, privilege which can be used to leverage resources and influence change in our own circles. Right? Skin color/complexion, wealth, education, connections, class position, etc. With all that's happened in 2020, we're way past looking wide-eyed and confused about our shared reality, way past being worried about compromising our own personal resources and reputation if we step forward to help. We're past pretending that we can't see how our privilege—and the refusal to use it to help others—increasingly feeds the disparities between us.

But also, it's time for the wounded among us to stop acting out, like they're the only ones on the planet who ever suffered and are thereby entitled to even the score, causing their own damage or inflicting their hurt onto another person. It's time. That kind of mentality and its ensuing actions are detriments to all of us. It undermines any progress we try to make towards bridging the gaps of understanding and leveling the playing field so that everyone can thrive.

Black people are the most loving, resilient, imaginative, and friendliest people I know. I met hundreds of them during my book research, complete strangers who readily opened hearts to me, who smiled easily, and answered survey questions. During query period, the strangers I met—in malls, on streets in working districts, in parking lots, in libraries, even in subway stations—chatted, offered wise commentaries, and also laughed with me. They nodded and they encouraged. I drew strength from such meetings.

And yet, those weren't the only kinds of Black people I met. In the Black community, among the challenges resulting from our painful history, we live with a hard truth that lingers over us like flammable, drifting fumes of gas. We shake our heads and make jokes about it like we're collectively helpless to nail it down for a solution. When we love, it's all good. *But when we hate, we come for each other first.* As strangers, whenever we are unknown to each other, some of us have been known to display a kind of distrust that borders on simmering hostility. When we don't know one of our own, there've been times when some of us gives that person a side-eye and stare-down which is just plain hateful. I was occasionally met with this kind of hostility during my research. It didn't happen often, but it happened enough to disrupt workflow and slow me down.

That's how we display our hostility in all-Black spaccs. In all-white spaces, we do a remix on the hostile presentation making our attitude less noticeable. We're deliberately subtle with stolen glances at peripheral gawking. Here, we ignore each other. In a room full of white people, we will talk with the white people and pretend we don't see the person who is Black, even if we are the only Black people in the room.

I know what this is. I've been a perpetrator of such irrational hostility to Black strangers myself in earlier seasons. It's caused by open wounds that are still hurting. You experience emotional pain and you don't want anyone else to hurt you, so you become distrustful. My dirty looks to other Blacks—when I was a younger woman—were to warn them off, to put up a defensive stance, and protect myself from potential negative approaches. I'm not proud that I was this way. I was stuck in my experience of being victimized by childhood trauma and reinjuries of the world. It was hard for me to see this about myself, but once I saw it, I couldn't keep it up without becoming a part of all the other problems which plague us as Blacks in America.

The younger generation is watching us for examples of how to navigate our racial tensions and the racially traumatizing experiences.

What's the answer? How do we handle this? I'm not sure. But I know how *not* to handle it. We can't meet hate with more hate and expect things to improve. Love is the best answer I know. Whatever *love* means for you, however it inspires you, go for it.

Everyone doesn't need to write a book about their experiences—unless of course, they want to, which I would love because way more interesting stories than mine are out here, not being told—but it doesn't make the experiences matter less. And just so we're clear, just because we get deliberate and start opening up about what's hurting us, doesn't mean that we live happily ever after and need never worry about pain again. Ha! I wish. Life is a journey. We're never done with learning and growing until we're dead. The stories we're telling and reading are the stories we're all still on the inside of, living.

Black women have continued to take numerous negative hits in various aspects of American culture. We're tired, I know. For the most part, I think most of us are staying positive and hopeful. But our connections to each other tend to be either frayed or fraught.

Not all of us are ready to talk about all the painful particulars which are getting in the way of our bonds as Black women, causing misunderstandings between and among us. So I went first by writing this book.

As I wrote in earlier pages here, friendships are just as intimate as any other partnership. And if there's a break in any bond and the parties involved are willing to repair the existing relationship or do the healing necessary to become better partners for a future pairing, we need to put in the work. Putting in the work means unpacking the mental baggage which has weighed us down and held us back from living our best lives.

I began with myself. I'm hoping this kind of start will give someone else the courage to trust a little extra and open up a little more. I know it's not easy. But we have daughters and granddaughters to think about; we are the examples they will want to follow. We really need to continue with carrying the legacy of Black womanhood which got us all here in the first place.

We are not our pain or our broken hearts. As Black women, we are more. As Black women, we deserve more. And we can have more whenever we're ready.

I stopped and connected the dots of my experiences. Connecting the dots unlocked the doors of my mind, revealing magic.

Dream-Chasing From The Margins is the book that needed to appear first. My writing journey unfolded exactly as it was meant to, just like my life so far. How can I reject any part of my life without rejecting who I am at my core? I embrace it all. Everything that happened to me—every heartbreak, every joy, every wound, every mistake, and every delightful thing—happened exactly as it should have. The cumulative seasons made me who I am today. I regret none of it.

Now I can move onto the next leg of this writing journey. Now I can finish writing the friendship book about Black women. This time, when fear or sadness comes for me again—which it surely will—I'll be ready to meet it and move through it because experience has shown, beautiful things often come after.

ACKNOWLEDGMENTS

For many years, before I got on the writer's journey, I would read the acknowledgments at the end of books with envy. This is because I'd gone so long—decade after decade—feeling unloved. But that was just the story that an abused little girl once narrated on repeat in her little brain for so long that it stuck. Now that I've given my wayward brain a reboot, I'm seeing myself and my life in a whole new way. The dust has settled and living is better. There are friends from my past and present to thank for the many ways they've blessed my life with their presence.

To my editor, Becky Smith, thanks for your tremendous work. I learned a lot by working with you.

To all the Black women who agreed to be surveyed and interviewed for my research into Black women's friendships. Your enthusiasm and encouragement about the friendship topic inspired me to keep going and never give up.

To my best friend of more than forty-five years, Charlene John King, thank you for being the sister I didn't know I needed, the sister who walked with me through many wild and epic times as we grew into full womanhood. You found me on one of the saddest days of my life; you took my hand and you never let go. Thanks to our friendship, I have excellent childhood memories that I will always cherish.

To my parents, thank you for giving me life. I'm clear now on how difficult life must have been for you both and on my understanding of the unhealed wounds you've each carried for so long. As fractured and as painful as our family ties became, I will always love and appreciate the life you gave me. You gave to me that which you knew how to give. I've taken your offerings and made it enough. You're more amazing than you were ever able to realize for yourselves. With the writing of this memoir, I am breaking the cycle of our generational curse.

To my siblings, we made it. Despite our divergent paths, I will always love you.

To my maternal and paternal grandmothers, Hilda Gordon and Ellen Barnes, I miss and love you dearly. Hilda, thank you for being the first woman to make me feel like a queen. Not only has those first five years of life in Jamaica never left my heart or my thinking, the dormant seeds of brilliance and self-belief you planted bloomed fifty years later, and life has become more beautiful than my biggest dreams. Ellen, thank you for showing me the scrappy fierceness, business acumen, and splendid love of a black woman who knows her own mind. It took some time, but I finally learned how to harness some of those admirable traits. I carry each of you in my heart.

To my business coach, Michelle Ward. Working with you was an incredible and magical gift from The Universe. The women I've known throughout life have tended to root for me quietly during our shared adulthood. You, Michelle, were the first woman to stand up with noise-makers, feet-stomping, and cheering every time we met and discussed my small victories. Wow. That meant a lot to me and added to my self-belief.

To my current therapist, Mary E. May, thank you for endorsing my desire to prioritize my own needs and put myself first. As women in the patriarchy, we sometimes fail to realize just how radical self-love can be. You helped me to stay on the self-love journey.

To my therapist (of an earlier season), Lisa Mawhinney, thank you for being there for me above and beyond a clinician's usual job duties. You were a great friend during my days as an office worker and you helped me to begin the arduous journey towards psychological and emotional healing.

To all my circles of friends from seasons past and current, thank you for the lessons you brought, for your generosity, and for your love. For the times spent together, you were each members of the family I got to choose.

My family ties multiplied due to two of my most cherished bonds, my husband and my childhood bestie. To the families who opened their arms and let me in, thank you for adopting me into your tribe. The Johns (Charlene's family). The Archers and Changs (the *best* in-laws a girl could ever hope for). I'm honored and elated to belong to such extraordinary groups of humans.

(Although I don't know these next three women personally, I owe them thanks for the hope and inspiration they've given me.)

To musical artists and businesswomen, Beyoncé Knowles Carter and Robin Rihanna Fenty—thank you for inspiring a fifty-something-year-old woman to step proudly into her sexuality. Women's bodies are too often policed under the intrusive gaze of patriarchy's foot soldiers, causing many of us to shrink and contort ourselves for approval. Your brave and beautiful music inspired a former victim of the predatory rape culture to reclaim her own body. Nowadays, I'm way less shy about radiating—even flaunting—my own sexual energy thanks to your imaginative songs and show-stopping performances. Ow! Black girls most definitely rock!

To Oprah Winfrey, business mogul, you are my forever she-ro. Thank you for paving so many roads for us all.

To my blog readers of past and present days, especially to the readers of the *On Becoming Maria* blog, thank you for following my journey. Thanks for your loyal readership. Your dedicated presence inspired me to keep writing.

To Brooklyn, the BEST borough in New York City. I love everything about you, including all the fellow crazies and lovelies of our teeming citizenry. You were my school of hard fucking knocks and I'm proud of every moment I lived through in your rough and tumble arms.

To my daughters, Tristen Norman and Nadhirah Norman—watching you grow from girlhood into womanhood has been the most astounding experience of my life. I'm so proud and truly honored to call myself your mother. Seeing how beautiful and brilliant you each became in your own right, stepping fully and independently into your own respective adulthoods, gave me the first indication that I actually did something special with my life. You two are my favorite she-roes, the two black women I admire the most in this world. When I think about game-changing millennials who are making The World a better place to live in, I see your faces. Thanks for patiently waiting as I figured out how to become a better mother. I love you both dearly.

To my husband, Howard Archer—in this extraordinary and devoted marriage, you've given me the BEST seventeen years of my life so far. Ward, you are my rock, my sweet lover, my business partner, and my bestest friend. This book could never have happened without you. You bore witness to an incredibly painful and arduous creative birth without blinking. You've been my biggest cheerleader for the entire book writing journey. You never stopped showing up and standing up for me. You were so understanding, giving up our weekends and some of our nights, allowing me as much time as I needed to write. You grocery shopped, washed dishes, did laundry, and stayed out of my way in order to let me write. You listened patiently whenever I needed to vent through frustrated tears, at times when the writing felt daunting, and threatened to overwhelm me. Each time my fears took me down this road of insecurity, you reminded me of my gifts and worthiness as a writer. And finally, Ward, you tirelessly read every page of this book over and over, helping with the edits and giving the most thoughtful and encouraging feedback. Thank you so much, baby. I love us and I love our team. This book is as much yours as it is mine.

APPENDIX

Book writing is a solitary journey. You spend many long hours alone. Some writers are fortunate to find online writing communities; or if they live in big cities, writers also have the privilege of belonging to writing groups where they gather and draw support from fellow creatives. I live in a fairly small and rural town in Pennsylvania, so my options were limited. As for the online groups, there are so many out there—*hundreds, actually*—to sift through. I haven't found the time yet to discover an online writing group which fits my needs. But I'm human and human beings are wired for connection. I like the way writer/therapist, Lori Gottlieb puts it in her book's acknowledgement page: we grow in connection to others. I created my own support community of artists through my passion for books and music. I couldn't list *all* the truth-telling writers and artists who inspired me and gave me courage throughout my life because there are so many of them. The following is a partial list (in no particular order) of some of my favorite artists and the work they produced which I leaned heavily on along my book writing journey.

Fiction Books
The Orchardist – Amanda Coplin
Little Fires Everywhere – Celeste Ng
The Care and Feeding of Ravenously
        Hungry Girls – Anissa Gray
The Emperor's Children – Claire Messud
Where the Crawdads Sing – Delia Owens
She Rides Shotgun – Jordan Harper
This Could Hurt – Jillian Medoff
Want – Lynn Steger Strong
American Dirt – Jeanine Cummins

Non-Fiction Books
All About Love: New Visions – bell hooks
Rock My Soul – Black and Self-Esteem
        bell hooks
Maybe You Should Talk to Someone – Lori Gottlieb
In Search of Our Mothers' Garden – Alice Walker
Between the World and Me – Ta-Nehisi Coates
Here For It – R. Eric Thomas
I Am Not Your Negro – James Baldwin, Raoul Peck
Bird by Bird – Anne Lamott
No Thanks: Black, Female, and Living In
        The Martyr-Free Zone
        Keturah Kendrick
My Time Among the Whites – Jennine Capó Crucet
Small Doses: Potent Truths for Everyday Use
        Amanda Seales
We're Going to Need More Wine
        Gabrielle Union
The Chronology of Water: A Memoir
        Lidia Yuknavitch
Not That Bad: Dispatches From Rape Culture
        Roxane Gay

No Happy Endings – Nora McInery
Sweetbitter – Stephanie Danler
*All The F*cking Mistakes: A Guide to Sex,
      Love and Life* – Gigi Engle
Women Who Run With Wolves
            Clarissa Pinkola Estés, Ph.D.
No One Tells You This – Glynnis MacNicol
The Gifts of Imperfection - Brené Brown
Rising Strong – Brené Brown
Breaking the Habit of Being Yourself
            Dr. Joe Dispenza
The Seat of the Soul – Gary Zukav
The Writing Life – Annie Dillard
The Creative Habit – Twyla Tharp
The Untethered Soul – Michael A. Singer
Sister Outsider – Audre Lorde
You Are A Badass – Jen Sincero
The Big Leap – Gay Hendricks
Wild – Cheryl Strayed
The Problem With Everything – Meghan Daum
The Rules Do Not Apply – Ariel Levy
The War of Art – Steven Pressfield
On Writing – Stephen King
Revolution From Within – Gloria Steinem
Good Things Happen to People You Hate
            Rebecca Fishbein
*Blackout: Remembering the Things I Drank
      To Forget* – Sarah Hepola
*Quit Like A Woman: The Radical Choice to
Not Drink In A Culture Obsessed With Alcohol*
            Holly Whitaker
Drink: A Love Story – Caroline Knapp

Songs
Feeling Good – Nina Simone
Lemonade, album – Beyoncé
Black Is King: The Gift, album – Beyoncé
I Am Light – India.Arie

Break The Shell – India.Arie
Strength, Courage, and Wisdom – India.Arie
Soldier of Love – Sade
The Big Unknown – Sade
Run The World (Girls) – Beyoncé
Ave Maria – Beyoncé
I'm Better – Missy Elliot
Orange Sky – Alexi Murdoch
It's Only Fear – Alexi Murdoch
Retrograde – James Blake
Just Like Fire – Pink
F*ckin' Perfect – Pink
IDGAF – Dua Lipa
Roots – Imagine Dragons
Yesterday – Imagine Dragons
Girl On Fire – Alicia Keys
New Day – Alicia Keys
Brand New Me – Alicia Keys
Under Dog – Alicia Keys
Good Job – Alicia Keys
So Done – Alicia Keys, Khalid
These Days – Angel Snow
Ain't No Sunshine – Bill Withers
Lovely Day – Bill Withers
Perfect Duet – Ed Sheeran, Beyoncé
Love Myself – Tracee Ellis Ross
Fight Song – Rachel Platten
Amen – Andra Day
Landslide – Dagny
You Don't Know About Me – Ella Vos
I Like That – Janelle Monáe
Life (Is What You Make It) – Frighty, Colonel Mite
Middle Finger – Cham
Big Things A Gwan – Daddy Screw, Donovan Steele
Adore You – Miley Cyrus
Nice For What – Drake
Warrior – Demi Lovato
Heart's Mystery – Nick Barber
Kelly – Kelly Rowland

The Bones – Maren Morris, Hozier
Never Give Up – Sia
Original – Sia
Icon – Jaden
Inner Peace – Beautiful Chorus
Akaal – Ajeet, Trevor Hall
Desperado – Rihanna
Pour It Up – Rihanna
Trumpets – Jason Derulo
White Flag – Dido
Hard Knock Life – Jay-Z
Drop The World – Lil Wayne

In Loving Memory

of

Wilma John-Redman
1943 – 2020

Thanks for reading!
Here are a few places you where you can find me to say hello
and stay in the loop for future books and content.

Website: miaharcher.com
Instagram: @writer.mia.h.archer
Twitter: @MiaHArcherWriter
mia.h.archer.writer@gmail.com

Made in the USA
Middletown, DE
08 March 2021